W9-AEC-037

WHen a WOMan Takes an axe TO a waLL

[WHERE IS SHE REALLY TRYING TO GO?]

Also by Allegra Bennett

Renovating Woman: A Guide to Home Repair,
Maintenance and Real Men

How to Hire A Contractor

WHEN a WOMAN TakES an axe TO a WaLL

[WHERE IS SHE REALLY TRYING TO GO?]

allegra bennett

www.renovatingwoman.com

The Writer's Lair Books

www.writerslairbooks.com

Copyright © 2006 by Allegra Bennett. All rights reserved under International and Pan-American Copyright Conventions. No part of this book may be reproduced or transmitted in any form or by any means, electronic or mechanical, including photocopying, recording, or by any information storage and retrieval system, without permission in writing from the copyright owner.

Published by
THE WRITER'S LAIR BOOKS
P.O. Box 44286
Nottingham, MD 21236
www.writerslairbooks.com

Book design by Sherin Nicole

ISBN: 0975440241

LCCN: 2006925972

The WRITERS'S LAIR BOOKS title and design are the registered trademarks of The Writer's Lair Books, Inc.

PRINTED IN THE UNITED STATES OF AMERICA

*Life is not about finding yourself
but creating yourself*

– a sign in a store window

contents

WHEN A WOMAN TAKES AN AXE...

[book two]
HARD HATS
49

WHEN A WOMAN TAKES AN AXE...

the universe delivers:
an introduction

Over the years, women have generously opened the books of their lives allowing me a peek at a few pivotal pages and grace notes. The similarities show that the universe delivers much the same adventures to each of us with absolutely no regard for the artificial barriers of education, class, age, ethnicity, sexuality, height, weight or gender.

I have faith in what women can do and I have faith in the promise of homeown**her**ship. It is prompting women to create workshops of their own in their basements, closets and sheds. They have their own tools. They can cite the strength of one brand over another. They can tell you where the bargains are, the after markets, and how to prolong the life of equipment and appliances.

They are in the stores, not just responding to the "Softer side of Sears" as the old ad goes, but taking advantage of Father's Day and Mother's Day sales to buy tools for themselves! Now there's a merchandising heads up— forget the gender focused 'nighties and necklaces for mom and ties and tools for dad' ads. *The ladies are getting power tool empowered!*

My first serious power tool was an electric chain saw with a 24 inch bar and removable power cord. I loved it. I first saw it during my victory shopping trip to Sears to celebrate repairing the garbage disposal *(more on that later)*. It had been years since I visited the store and for the first time I went directly to the tool department to stock up on how-to gadgets. I was, after all, a bona fide do-it-yourself homeowner. *I had fixed something!* I felt I belonged there, even though the sales clerks, male and female, assumed I was buying "a gift for the hubby."

It was a few weeks after my Sears trip that I actually bought the chain saw, this time at a home improvement store. It seemed that every week, just like the guys I saw there, I was walking somebody's tool aisle. In fact, I had gotten so into tool and gadget ownership that on day one of the grand opening of a new home improvement store near me, I packed salad, fruit and beverages, and spent the entire day there. I prowled the aisles marveling at all the stuff that would make my life as a serial fixer a joy— and I wasn't the only woman in the place. There were others making trips as regularly as I was. *And they weren't just buying plants.*

The stories and perspectives you will find here represent the experiences of many women, and *somewhere here you will find you.*

HOUSE
POWER

...the moment one definitely commits oneself,
Providence moves too...
Whatever you can do, or dream you can do, begin it.
Boldness has genius, power, and magic in it.

Begin it now.

– Goethe

one.
an anthropological dig

Every woman who engages a wall with the serious edge of an axe isn't just trying to get to the other side. Feminine motivation and destination are never all that obvious. Even the tools used are misleading as to the mission. Indeed, she may take down a wall, or dress it up with fresh paint or paper. For that matter, she may hang new drapes, sand and polish the floors or move the furnishings around. But where this woman is heading is a space far more lasting than the decorative touches and renovation changes. The task at hand often serves double duty as an unexpected but inevitable meditation zone from which she will emerge enriched, with clarity of purpose and a luminous understanding of who she really is.

On one level or another, all humans engage in a treasure hunt for their authentic self. It is a perpetual search that, in the case of women, is typically obscured by our focus on seeing to other people's needs.

Along the journey from girlhood to womanhood we begin early looking away from ourselves. Our attention is deflected by roles to play: the good daughter, loving spouse, nurturing mother and/or devoted caretaker. We raise children, grow careers and care for aging parents. We rise to the need performing the roles serially or all at once, seldom pausing long enough to probe the critically important question: "Who is Me?" And that question is no minor selfish inquiry. The answer defines why we are here.

Throughout the ages, humankind has groped about for the answer to "Who is Me?" The insistent demand for self-discovery is an intuitive curiosity that can be tracked from toddler to teenager and beyond. What two-year-old follows orders not their own? It's the year of the 'No!' expressed without reservation and backed by stiffened bodies and food stuff tossed from the high chair.

By the teen years 'I'm trying to find myself' becomes the mantra of the day. Heartfelt as that plea is, few grown ups can resist playing it for laughs with the dismissive, 'You'd better find yourself in your room and clean it up.' Marriage creates a new kind of territorial stakeout that is often articulated by pronouncements such as "we're growing apart," "you're not hearing me," or some other such clue that this clueless partnership needs attention. No matter what the age, we all are driven to discover, serve and protect the territory known as 'Me'.

For a woman, the journey to *Me* typically gets derailed, leaving her original self to wait for later discovery. Ironically, divorce, death, financial ruin or catastrophic illness come along as cloud covered detours providing the pause that becomes a useful tool for self excavation–*depending on how we look at it.*

Meanwhile, a woman's life fills with metaphors. She takes an axe to a wall and creates the opening between the kitchen and the dining room that she 'always wanted.' She strips paper from the walls trying to get to something sure. She scrapes away layers of paint from wood moldings and furniture to get down to the basics. Having reached the first stop in this deconstructive phase, she applies whatever treatment she desires. Paint it. Paint it not.

Tearing down to build back up is unmistakable symbolism. It is an anthropological dig, exploring and fundamentally recovering the meaning of a life during the highly meditative act of renovating and loving a space. *When a woman takes an axe to a wall* — in whatever form it takes — it's to clear away buildup and uncover the foundation of her real self, where ultimately she uplifts her space and her spirit.

*"I have learned that my heart's desire
is in my own home and in my own front yard."*

— Dorothy in the Wizard of Oz

two.
'ann wiff' et al

When I was married I used to chuckle when the water and annual property tax bills arrived in the mail. Buying the house was my idea and the purchase happened primarily on the strength of my income and work history, yet my name was written nowhere on the bill. Right after my husband's name on the address line was the allusive extension "and WF," an abbreviation that summarily disenfranchised me as it does hundreds of thousands of other women so identified. The municipal bill collectors couldn't even bring themselves to spell out "wife." So, for the twelve years we owned the house together my name, as decided by the city of Baltimore, was 'Ann Wiff'.

It was not until I was divorced, and had to refinance the property, that I got a name and of course it was only half mine since the formal part of it belonged to *you know who*. I'm not complaining mind you, just making written note of the points along the social trail where the marginalization of a woman gets its reinforcement.

Despite little episodes like 'Ann Wiff', the perception of what a woman wants and is capable of achieving for herself and society at large is changing. A great place for collecting anecdotal evidence about what women are up to is at the local home improvement stores where women aren't just signing up for decorating tips at those free classes being offered. They are going for the gold. They want to demystify plumbing, electricity, the workings of a house. They want to acquire the knowledge for trouble shooting and replace toilets themselves. They want to swap out old faucets, install dimmer switches, and replace light fixtures and switches themselves. These women demand to know what they need to know. They want their questions taken seriously and answered completely. They harbor a pent up demand to fill the box with tools they can use and take the care and feeding of their homes into their own hands.

Who are these demanding women? They are a dynamic mix across every demographic category, some of whom showed up in sharp evidence early one spring morning at the first *Renovating Woman* do-it-HERself workshop.

The event was a brainstorm I had one day after years of answering home improvement questions online from visitors to the renovating-woman.com web site and in my quarterly magazine Renovating Woman. I went through hundreds of questions and identified interests that translated into workshops that could provide women the answers they needed.

While I knew there was a need, no one was prepared for the response the day of the event. I was grateful I had witnesses in the form of the few sponsors who believed in the idea and pitched in

when a woman takes an axe...

money, talent and time to help. There was a pre-registration requirement but more than double the registration had come through that day. The women began lining up at the gate at 7 AM for the all-day event that was scheduled to begin at 8 AM. By 7:30 the parking lot was jammed with cars and lines of participants stretched from the door, through the parking lot, onto the sidewalk and around the corner. The attendees had come from Massachusetts, New Jersey, Pennsylvania and Washington, D.C. These women were serious and hungry for information. I am glad I had witnesses to this phenomenon.

The energy that morning is a reflection of the activity in the home-buyer market where homeown*her*ship, as I like to call it, is exploding. For a bit of logic let's go to the statistics.

According to housing industry reports, of all the households headed by women, 54 percent are homeowners. The U.S. Department of Housing and Urban Development statistics show that more than one-third of the recent increases in homeownership rates are due to gains by women. In fact, homeown*her*ship is increasing at a faster rate than the entire country–having risen 5 percent since 1994. Some of this growth is thanks to programs established within the last decade to make ownership easier for the so-called non-traditional mortgage holding population of women, minorities and low-income families.

Bringing women and homes together in ownership is a terrifically smart idea. As it is, in almost every consumer sector, women rule. They drive the consumer product market, influencing selections and the decision to buy. In cars, it's their choice of color, number of doors and creature comfort options. In houses, it's their decision about location, the size of the kitchen, number of bathrooms and the color of the paint on the walls.

Women are the ones in the grocery stores making the choices that stock the cupboards at home and in the retail shops deciding what the family will wear and what curtains will hang from the windows. Women's needs and desires are influencing the homebuilder market, where homes are being designed and constructed based on what she is asking for. You can bet that placing the laundry room on the same level as bedrooms - as is the case in many new constructions - was influenced by she who does the laundry. For a person with that much power, homeown*her*ship is an obvious privilege long overdue.

A home purchase is the single largest purchase most people will make in a lifetime. It plants for the owner a psychological stake in the ground and an intoxicating sense of self worth and belonging. Call it soul equity. What's more, for women there is a natural synergy with a house. Women are finding in homes not only a place to reside but an extension of her protective and nurturing nature.

Houses and women even share similar qualities. Both provide shelter emotionally and physically for those who enter their space. Both absorb pain and joy and can be temperamental or fussy. Both require attention and can be famously unforgiving if allowed to go uncared for and unloved for any length of time. Both are rewarding when lovingly attended. Both can bring out the best in the other–*or the worst.*

The psychological relationship between a house and its dweller did not escape the attention of famed behavioral psychologist Carl G. Jung and his followers. James Yandell, former president of the C.G. Jung Institute of San Francisco notes "Nesting, home-making, is a major means of personal expression and development. We create our immediate environment and then contemplate it and are worked on by it. We find ourselves mirrored in it, see what had been not yet visible and integrate the reflection back into our sense of self."

Any woman who has created a success knows this sweet space in her spirit. Her accomplishment may be shelves she installed on the wall—*straight;* a book case she built; a room she painted; a lamp she fixed or just the attainment of some goal she was uncertain she could manage and through that the establishment of her own identity.

This 'realization through renovation' proves that for women, houses are more than bricks and mortar. They are a supremely nurturing shelter, much like a mother's womb.

three.
home alone

Divorce and widowhood have been the typical entry-way to first-time, solo homeown*her*ship for many women. That's how it was for me. I got the house in the divorce. It was not the best part of the deal.

The house was a half-century old stucco-over-wood-frame Victorian, located in a stable, vibrant neighborhood. It featured a three-quarter wrap around porch, a deck, four bedrooms, a living room, formal dining room, eat in kitchen, attic and basement and was situated on a lot with front, back and side yards with lots of grass. For a dozen years, it was the Ponderosa where my husband and I raised our son and daughter and sealed the finale of our twenty-three years of marriage.

What I didn't know as a wife I discovered as a divorcee. The place had issues. The house was a hypochondriac. There was always something mechanically or physically amiss. The roof needed surgery, the outside walls and trim needed a face-lift, the basement needed plugging and the plumbing constantly demanded alternate doses of curatives to relieve the bouts of nausea and constipation in the pipes. I wasn't cognizant of this stuff while I was married. I didn't have to be. A man was at home. He was the fix-it quarterback and I had no desire to run interference.

Had it occurred to me that I would have to do my own repairs, I would have insisted he take the house in the divorce. Then I could have been the one to go live in a condo with a concierge in the lobby and twenty-four hour, on-call maintenance service. However, it didn't happen that way. In fact, The Ex didn't even put up a fight for the house. He just let me have it. *Smart move on his part.* But I am not unhappy. At least not now.

Back then the house started out feeling like a place of confinement and unending expenditures, but it evolved into an institution of perpetual learning. I learned all of its systems, what it liked and didn't like, its vulnerabilities, how to do repairs, major and minor, and perform maintenance routines to keep the misadventures down to a minimum. In that process I discovered a part of myself that was far more sufficient and brave than I had practiced being. That self forged a career I would never have thought of for me in a hundred life times.

Home alone for the first time in my life, my first conscious observation about my little abode was that the neighborhood squirrels and pigeons had worked a deal and developed the roof into an equal opportunity co-op. They used the rotting fascia boards of the overhang as their main and rear entrances to the eaves. These guys were early risers. The squirrels had frequent family disputes. They settled them by chasing each other around the space in the eaves, producing thunderous sounds like greyhound dogs on a race track running with cement blocks on their feet.

When the furry ones were done with their day of gathering and hunting in the neighborhood, they used the arching tree branches to springboard their way back home, landing with a clump into the roof. The pigeons flapped around noisily in the gutters and atop the downspouts and left gift deposits of guano that stained the windows and concrete below. It was months before I did anything about these squatters. I didn't know where to start. Call an exterminator, the ASPCA, the Zoo, what?

I eventually figured out the first call I needed to make was for a carpenter. But first, there was my adventure with the garbage disposal, the pivotal, life-changing experience in my life. This appliance was my first fix-it challenge and my first triumph, a simple task that became a seminal act in discovering the real Allegra.

From the time we had it installed, the garbage disposal did not work properly. Anything you put in it from potato skins to air, backed up and flooded the basement every time we used it. After a while we just stopped using it. I was shoving shrimp heads down the hopper the morning I remembered that important fact. The sound of water splashing in the basement triggered the recall. It had backed up again.

During the marriage my role in garbage disposal repair was minimal. I merely followed orders my husband yelled to me from his post in the basement. My job was to position a plunger over the drain in the kitchen sink and fill it with water. I'd hold the plunger in place until he yelled upstairs for me to let it go. I am yet clueless about what he did down there in the basement. I wasn't curious and didn't ask. All that mattered was when he re-emerged the disposal was working—until the next time.

So having forgotten this appliance was unreliable, I turned it on. Upon hearing the splash, I reacted to 23 years of conditioned response, panicked and reached for the phone to call the former man of the house for help. His advice did not ease my fears. He said I would have to aerate, get a balance of oxygen in the pipes and—*hey throw horse-shoes*—I didn't know what he was talking about. In any event I would accomplish this major plumbing feat by snaking the main drain. I would have to do this! Other than knowing the main drain was in the basement I had no idea how to recognize it. And I wasn't going to open some hatch to release creatures that would pop and scare the life out of me.

I thanked him, hung up and reached for the Yellow Pages. However, the plumbers' prices for an in-home consultation provided the reality check that sent me to the basement looking around the floor for this main drain myself. Imagine my surprise to find the drain coming out of the wall about eye level. Seated in the drain was a black rubber hose. I figured out by deductive reasoning *(I looked)* that it was the water take out line leading from the underside of the dishwasher. We had stopped using the brand new dishwasher after a few uses, for the same reason we stopped using the garbage disposal—it backed up. *(You'd gag too if there was a rubber hose stuffed down your throat with no room for air to pass let alone a meal.)*

All along, the problem was the black rubber hose, which was too long and was choking the drain. I deduced that shortening the hose would solve the problem. So I shortened it, inserted it back in position, clamped it in place, went upstairs to the kitchen, crossed my fingers and turned on the water and flipped the switch for the disposal.

It worked. No backup. Just free flow. I was completely giddy. I, me, myself had provided a permanent repair to a mechanical problem that had my household vexed and stumped for some time. And the amazing thing was the fix was a no-brainer. Just common sense. Logic. Just taking a look!

The Ex was not home when I called him back with the great results so I left a detailed message on his answering machine, mentioning the black hose. Then I did the only thing a gal must do to celebrate: I went out on a shopping spree. To buy tools. After all, if I was going to be fixing stuff, I needed the tools to do it, and the electric drill, the set of screwdrivers, slip joint pliers and 25 foot retractable tape measure would get me started.

I thought I was hot stuff. I could smell my feminine level of testosterone and now knew the intoxicating feeling of cockiness. That one success was a major breakthrough that left me curious and confident. I wanted to know how everything worked and how to fix it all myself. I was on my way to becoming a serial fixer.

Upon my return home from my tool buying trip, I retrieved a message from the telephone answering machine the Ex left while I was out. "Oh," he said "that's what that black hose was." It was clear from his response he never really investigated the source of the disposal problem. So the question became what was he doing in the basement all those times when we were "fixing" the thing. I had to laugh. And I understood.

I also came to understand why I automatically relinquished the fix-it tasks to him, taking no leadership role for myself. The answer in part is subconscious conditioning on both our parts. A woman's subconscious is so primed for failure with unfamiliar tasks that without trying we conclude the fix is difficult and beyond us. Consequently, we seek the expertise of someone who "everyone" takes for granted has intuitive knowledge of such things–men. We concede our options early in the game and somewhere along our development, women got indelibly imprinted with those lasting cultural myths of inferiority and incompetence.

The effect of cultural myths is that even today we yield to a host of supposed no no's and self-select out of an array of male-designated etceteras. There is a corresponding myth for males: Men are supposed to know it all. The fact that they don't puts pressure on them to come up with answers. So you end up with a spouse in the basement masquerading his way through a repair for years.

In his provocative novel, *Ishmael*, author Daniel Quinn raises the phenomenon of the cultural myth, that is, the operative story about our society we all accept as true. Without knowing it, I adopted the prevailing belief that there is men's work and women's work. It was just one of those subliminal messages that was reinforced a thousand ways and stuck in my psyche as it sticks in the subconscious of millions of women.

These myths adjust with each generation and individual experience. But they remain indelible as long as there is reinforcement through advertisement, entertainment and other subliminal vehicles that ultimately perpetuate stereotypes. That homeown*her*ship is growing signals that these myths are losing their power.

"I'll Believe It When I See It.
I'll See It When I Believe It"

four.
shelley's chalet

I had an amazing encounter with a woman I met on a train ride from Boston to Baltimore. The train was still in Boston's Back Bay station and I had just taken a seat by the window. A moment later, a voice with a question, "Anyone sitting here?." "Why, yes," *I answered theatrically,* "You." We both laughed at the spoken and unspoken humor in that moment. The Voice had passed a dozen or more completely empty aisles before reaching the one I was seated in. It was as if our *energy sensors* vibrated ahead of us in the train car, seeking a connection and found one. It was instantly clear that we were strangers in name only. Sitting anywhere but together would be unnatural. Our energy was so compatible over the long trip that others thought we were traveling together. And, of course we were. It felt like we had known each other forever.

After settling in, the Voice opened the newspaper she had brought along. We both took note of a story in the home section about the growth of women as do-it-yourselfers. It fueled our conversation. I told her that women do-it-HERselfers was the population I wrote for. As we talked we bonded further over the subject of houses and self-discovery. We both had stories to tell. Hers was still fresh for her. She opened up, talking on as if she had been waiting a long time for the opportunity. The Voice's name was Shelley.

Shelley had been married since she was 19 years old and was a wife and homemaker nearly all her adult life. She raised four sons who had their own families now and were living on their own. When she was 54 years old, her husband left her for a woman 20 years younger. Shelley dubbed her "the teen tart." Shelley was left with the house but no income. On her own and without any skills she recognized or valued as marketable — the divorcee, with the hazel eyes and the face of one of Raphael's painted cherubs, felt discarded and desperate.

Her home was in Michigan in a picturesque community that enjoyed great snowy seasons eight months of the year and gorgeous spring like weather, that lingered the remaining months. There were always students and couples visiting the area looking for an inexpensive place to stay for a day or two of hitting the slopes. They were a familiar sight while her sons were growing up. Those years were vibrant and it seems her boys always had friends visiting overnight.

Memory of those times came to Shelley one morning as she lay in bed staring into space, still tired from a sleepless night of money worries. The sound of the refrigerator's ice maker brought back the memories. When her sons had their friends over the refrigerator couldn't make ice fast enough. The crew seemed always thirsty and hungry. She marveled at how she managed to keep the human trash compactors, *as she called them*, fed and happy and watered. Shelly recalled how she teased "This is not a Chalet." As she lay there the words streamed across her mind, like a message on an electronic billboard then froze, prompting a smile and a question "What if...?"

Shelley couldn't remember when she ever lived alone. She was still at home with her parents when she got married and as a wife and mother there was always someone around needing her for one thing or another. She never really planned for life alone. There was the life insurance if her husband died. But divorce came with no financial benefits. It left her without means.

What made her smile was the thought of renting out two of the bedrooms in her house to the skiers who frequented the area. Although intriguing, the idea of strangers in her house still unnerved her somewhat. And how would she let the public know she had rooms to rent. She couldn't afford an ad and really did not want to put one in the newspapers or hand out flyers on the street. It all felt a little unclean and the idea of asking for money was so difficult for her. She sat up in bed and reached for the telephone to call one of her sons. Talking with him about it made her feel better about the idea, made it feel real and gave her courage, she said. It could work. The house was big enough.

Understanding her reluctance–and theirs–to advertising or floating flyers, her sons tapped their *old and new friend's network* and word spread about the rooms. Within a few weeks, Shelley started getting calls and overnighters trickled in. She provided towels and soap and offered a continental breakfast, although she didn't call it that. To her it was coffee, tea, orange juice, bagels and toast - things that came with a price tag. The provisions were simply a make-do, since she felt obliged to offer something. To keep her costs down she provided no mid-day meal and no dinner.

As a wife and mother, Shelley was part of a circle of women who were homemakers and frequently socialized together. But her status as a divorcee was unfamiliar to them and they felt threatened as if it might rub off on them. So now divorce also included another loss - separation from the group that had been her social grounding all of her married life. Renting out rooms in her house brought her further isolation. Her friends were uncomfortable and "embarrassed for her." They made themselves scarce. But in backing away, the women systematically took with them a critical undergirding for a woman in distress - the spiritual support of the sisterhood circle.

Some of the women let her know in uncertain terms they did not like her "shameful borders and renters" situation for their community. Their awkward encounters produced awkward comments. In a kinder gesture, one woman made a passing reference to the rentals as a "bed and breakfast." The words resonated and took on an empowering tone in her mind. They set her to really think about her house as a "cute little bed and breakfast." And, why not? She had nothing to lose. Shelley began dreaming about her two room rentals as an exclusive B&B.

At that point, it certainly was exclusive as a word of mouth venture. She clipped pictures of pretty room settings from magazines. Her focus on her new project provided the side benefit of relief from her embarrassment and fear over her situation. Shelley started holding her place in higher regard and worked at reinventing her house as an elegant retreat. "Once I saw it, I believed it. Once I believed it, I could see it," she said.

The budding innkeeper revisited an old footlocker filled with long-forgotten childhood memorabilia. She pulled out pretty picture frames, dainty embroidered doilies, lace sofa scarves and table runners she saved from her girlhood. She had packed them away upon the arrival of the second of her four sons. She revived the treasures and arranged them in the rooms. The space came alive with their heirloom accessories and a feeling of cozy warmth and loving settled within. The whole house felt like it was wearing a smile, she said.

With her surroundings now lovely, Shelley's attitude and view of the world brightened. She was energized and no longer saw the short-term rentals as a desperate solution but as a long, empowering step into the future. She created receipts, opened a checking account, wrote out a plan for growth and started viewing herself as a business-woman. She tapped into what she knew. And what she knew was how to provide comfort and service. She changed the menu and started cooking again from scratch.

She provided a hearty morning meal with a choice of cereals, pancakes and eggs and fresh fruit. Being the matriarch of a family of five males, she knew how to cook big. Her nurturing nature gently unfolded once again. Interestingly, the woman who was sheepish about asking people to pay to stay in her home, began to see value in what she offered. She eventually came to understand the connection between value and market price and was able to ask for the kind of fees she needed to really make her enterprise work without apology. After a time, she was able to hire an assistant to help with the chores that kept the place busy everyday of the week.

Shelley's warm hospitality inspired word-of-mouth that drew people who learned about 'not a cheap place to stay' but a 'lovely escape in a loving space'. They told their friends. Soon, the two guest rooms spread to four of the five bedrooms and for some years afterward Shelley ran her house as a quiet, thriving bed and breakfast that brought her a real income and a new life.

Shelley's own analysis of her success' reveals the obvious. Her house provided a source of practical financial support. Her experience as a nurturing mother and wife had value in a world where service is taken for granted. She was her greatest option and that fact became clear to her once she stopped looking back.

Planning and preparing the space so that it worked for her provided the distraction that helped her make peace with the past, accept the present and create a future in her new reality as a single woman. Looking ahead also provided an important shift in questions from "Why me?" to "Now what?" The process of working out the details of that answer transformed this accidental innkeeper from clutching and fearful to open and hopeful. Facing her fears and working through them was the *axe* that broke through a wall that had built up invisibly over a lifetime. The breakthrough brought her face to face with the woman on the other side—her vibrant self, the woman who led her home.

*"As a woman you have got to dust yourself off.
If you make a mistake fix it.
Apologize to any one you have hurt.
Apologize to yourself and keep moving."*

– Betty Jean Murphy

five.
value

Where Shelley could not immediately recognize and appreciate the marketplace value of her experiences as a wife, mother and homemaker, Betty Jean Murphy was always aware of her worth. She was good at making a room look pretty and inviting on a budget. She shopped the flea markets and after market sales to outfit her home even when she didn't have to. Then things changed. She was 38 years old with four children from ages 3-13 when she was divorced. "I lived in the house of my dreams." Things were just the way she wanted it. The kids were happy. The house was huge.

But her former husband was not willing to support her and their children in that house. Energy costs were high and became a major issue so they were forced to move. She received half the proceeds of the sale of the house and used it and her knowledge as a residential real estate agent to find a place for her and the children. "I bought a crummy house, a fixer upper. Four bedrooms and the ugliest kitchen in America," she said. She had always been a 'junker,' buying at flea markets. She sold some of the furnishings and doodads she collected and used the money to buy designer wallpaper to decorate.

Betty was intent on minimizing the disruption of the children. To keep their surroundings as familiar as possible the house she bought was just down the block. They had to pass their former residence on their way to their new home and it hurt. Upset with the changed circumstances, one of her children asked her if they were really going to live in the fixer upper. Her young daughter provided her sibling with a soothing answer based on her experience: "Mommy will fix it up. She'll make it beautiful."

Making things beautiful is Betty Jean's gift. She noticed that "Many times people view middle class women who can decorate and fix as a worthless thing. Having great taste is not seen as a value." But she knows the importance of surroundings and she made the creation of good surroundings the ideological foundation of Savannah Development Corporation, a company she created to build affordable housing for low and middle income residents.

"When my kids felt out of sorts I would tell them to go clean their room. I knew this would give them a sense of control once it was put in order." When she looked at the kind of carelessly designed and decorated rental housing that was created for the poor and working poor populations she realized a main ingredient was missing that kept residents from taking care of the place they lived. "Where you live and how you are treated impact how you live." Betty Jean committed herself to putting a product on the market that would be a part of social change. "Take the same financing and do more than just shelter people," she said.

After concluding she would never be a manager in the real estate business she got together with three other women and started a company. Each focused on the strength they brought to the table, acquisition, selling, paperwork and renovation. While married, Betty Jean always took care of the fix it chores, so renovation fell to her. "I was good at finding workers. I was not good at hammering and nailing, myself, but conceptualizing and finding someone who could make it work the way I wanted it to work."

When the partnership ended some years later Betty Jean reorganized, on her own, with her strengths providing the company's working capital. Her Savannah Development Corporation looks for opportunities to create the kind of housing she feels people deserve — affordable and beautiful housing are not mutually exclusive. Betty Jean is working her belief that providing such desirable housing for the poor is not only possible but necessary. Her company has created dozens of houses throughout the city of Baltimore. Some have the exclusive look of a gated community, but they are located in economically depressed areas of the city. "It is the best product, the most competitive and a niche development," she says.

The Good Witch of the North teaches that if you run away, your problems will run after you.

– Florence Scovel Schinn

six.
free me

Every now and then my subconscious sends me a message which I try to capture immediately in writing, using whatever blank space I can find nearby—the back of an envelope, a corner of a document, the palm of my hand, a napkin. In the last two years of my marriage and through the first year of divorce *(circa 1990-1993)*, one message kept popping up with the insistence of a revolutionary chant. It was a message that brought voice to an indescribable sense of something I had for at least a dozen years earlier. The message was powerful and succinct: "Free Allegra."

I scribbled the words everywhere creating a menagerie of Post-Its and paper scraps tucked in books or lying loose in the pockets of coats, seldom used purses, and briefcases. A review of scores of my old reporter's notebooks revealed the words "Free Allegra" doodled on pages as headlines and scattered throughout interviews. Apparently, during a particularly mind-numbing interview, I launched the

"Free Allegra Movement," judging by the underscoring, circling and heavy tracing of the words etched into the page.

While I was uncertain how I would set myself free, I had always sensed there existed another Allegra within me. I called her "laughing Allegra," after the little girl in Henry Wadsworth Longfellow's poem, *The Children's Hour*. The time had arrived to bring her forth. It was not so much physical freedom I was going for as the emancipation of spirit and my authentic self.

Actually, the other Allegra had shown up a few times before, making a series of visits to me on the job, but I always put her in check. *I had to*. She would be nothing but trouble for me if I let her out. However, she was persistent.

As a court reporter for the Baltimore Sun early in my journalism career, my duties took me to the U.S. District Court building everyday. The office there was a closet-sized space with a desk, typewriter, telephone and room for just one person. One afternoon I shut the door to review the cases I would turn into stories for the next day and the other Allegra showed up. I didn't physically see her but her presence was unmistakable. *And she had an attitude.*

This Allegra's personality was so strong, I gave her a name of her own–**Lila**. She was sassy, comical, self-assured, tart-tongued and hankering to be set loose on the world. I felt like a mere shadow of her. She told me she wanted to be released. I told her I could not meet her demand. *There was no way I could take that woman home.* I'd never be able to explain her. She was a carefree, daring, uncompromising, nonconformist personality. I was uptight and married then and my husband most assuredly would have thought I either lost my mind or was having an affair. I had to keep that gal under wraps. However, Lila threatened that if I didn't voluntarily set her free she would simply come out. She said she would take over my mind and body because she was not going to remain cooped up in a timid psyche. I made a deal: I'd let her out gradually.

Other women face this same dilemma. They know that the person they consciously present to the public is not the woman in full. Women are comprised of multiple personalities, some so distinct they need their own names to keep them straight. As the host of this convention of personalities, we're not always savvy about how to manage these gals. We let them out for an occasional romp when they insist, but for the most part keep them suppressed and away from the masses, away from ourselves.

The hybrid self we present in public is safe. She is that functional personality who is shaped by and conforms to society's comfort level and its definition of what individuals should be as members of a group. Women typically mistake their group identity for that of their authentic self until something happens to make them think.

I knew the 'Free Me' notes I found were urgent messages, and the time had come to discover myself. The oddest thing is to realize that more than forty years of my life had gone by and there still was something interesting, magical and of depth to discover about me. For at least 25 of those years I had focused on family and career and my context within those categories. Before then I was trying to please my mother and father and an assortment of teachers and employers. But I had never focused on the essence of me and the gifts I was born with that make me and each of us so unique. Until I found the notes I did not realize there was a difference and so much more to learn.

The light dawned the morning I was reorganizing storage and closet spaces to suit a bachelorette. A few days earlier my husband had completed his move out of the house as did our son who was beginning his first year in college and our daughter who moved to her new life in New York. Everyone who defined me was gone. The woman who was wife and mother was positioned center stage feeling like a cast member with no role to play.

I came across a series of 'Free Me' notes tucked between the pages of several books. I stared at the collection for some time, marveling at how many there were. I counted out eleven. I sure didn't remember writing them all. Over the next few months I would discover more. Notes in hand, I went to the full-length mirror and stared at all of me. "Free Allegra? Who is she? What she be about?" as my West Indian immigrant mother would pose the question. It was important for me to ask the question, to put it out there into the universe. I knew the answer would come.

Although divorce ultimately came at my insistence, the fact that it had to occur blind sided me. The concept never came up in all the years we were married. Even when there were serious challenges to the partnership, neither of us ever discussed breaking up. In fact, the very word *divorce* was never a part of our vocabulary, neither in jest or reckless threat. We went through difficult times but I saw them as temporary with us getting over the hurdles and settling down in twin glider rockers on a balcony in some warm climate keeping track of sunsets in our sunset years.

At least, that's a picture I painted in conversation. But I can't honestly say I believed it thoroughly. I could not really picture it in my mind's eye. The idea of idling away my senior years, any years, was antithetical to my nature. That much I knew. There had to be something more alive and affirming to look forward to than a pine rocking chair which in my mind was the vestibule to that final resting place in a pine box. I was not to discover there was another way to thinking about my life until I was single and holding those notes.

The message to "Free Me" was a subconscious clarion call to bring forth Lila, et al and set them free. I paid attention. *And, oh boy, do I love them.* I have no regrets. As a friend who recognized a profound change in me said to me once: "Have a great day. All of y'all."

"We have these instincts which defy all our wisdom and for which we never can frame any laws ... They are powers which are imperfectly developed in this life, but one cannot help the thought that the mystery of this world may be the commonplace of the next."

– Sarah Orne Jewett (1877)

seven.
it's alive!

We've all stepped into a room where we could just feel the tension or felt inexplicably at ease just upon entering. Whether we live spread out in all eighteen rooms of a fabulously drafty mansion or huddle-up in a one-room lean-to, the space where we do our most intense living is the catchall of our emotions.

Houses hold way more than furniture, people and boxes of forgotten doodads. They hold breath, the anger, sorrow, joy, depression, love or hatred expressed and experienced within their walls. But where do all the feelings go? Do they pile up in a corner of a room like dirty laundry or settle like dust onto the furniture, the walls, the floors, the ceiling, behind the radiators. Do they simply evaporate or do they roam around forever agitated in certain rooms? What about those personalities who cross over to the next life with issues of this life unresolved. Are they stuck in a space until they are released? I don't know.

What I do know is we must be mindful of what we set free within our space.

It would be interesting to know what went on in the house my young friend Sonia Hobbs bought before she arrived there as its new owner. For years, I tried convincing her to become a homeowner. She was in her mid-30's, single with a sizable, steady income and a teen-aged daughter she planned to send to college. I figured a house would be a good investment for her and I knew the psychological and spiritual benefits of owning your own. A home of her own would offer the growth I sensed she was seeking and I felt the time was right. But for most of her adult life, Sonia preferred giving her tax breaks to her landlord. She simply found security and flexibility in living the life of a renter. Her reasoning was "When something breaks down I can call the landlord to fix it. And if it can't be fixed I can move somewhere else."

However, there came a time when her thinking changed. I was pleasantly surprised when Sonia announced she was buying her first house. It was a roomy three-bedroom townhouse with a finished basement, den and tiled patio and garden out back. She was ecstatic when she moved in. However, the honeymoon was over in a week, after she began noticing a problem. It was not the kind of problem a landlord or maintenance staffer could necessarily correct. And it was nothing that could have been picked up in a home inspection. However, it explained why the previous owner was so anxious to sell after living there less than a year. The house appeared to have a ghost.

No matter what your beliefs about ghosts, the after-life or the spirit world, we all have experienced entering a room and feeling the presence of someone else. Usually, it was someone mortal whom we could see and touch, but just hadn't noticed right away. In Sonia's case the presence was not seen but felt, heard, and left evidence behind.

The spirit living there seemed to be partial to the kitchen and the main bedroom. It made itself known any time of the day and also kept late hours. Sonia said its activity included stomping up the stairs wearing what sounded like soft soled bedroom slippers. It hung around and routinely roused her and her sister from a deep sleep at 3:00 AM. It disapproved of Sonia's musical tastes and in fits changed the station selections to gospel channels, on the kitchen and car radios.

Sonia blamed the spirit for the flushing sound in the toilet and the blinking light on the telephone that occurred whenever a male guest visited the house. The blinking and flushing stopped once the guest left. A careful housekeeper, Sonia noticed that some days when she came home from work the magnets on the refrigerator had been rearranged.

As you might imagine, Sonia said she limited who she shared her ghost story with, fearing someone would think she was losing her mind. She was starting to think maybe she was. Then came collaboration from family and friends who stayed over a few nights. "They all heard it and felt what I had been experiencing," she said.

This first-time homeowner had just about had it with the lady of her manor role. She was ready to abandon the place and no one could blame her. But as a last effort she decided to have the house blessed by a priest. She noticed a peace afterwards but it didn't last long, she said. The energy returned, boldly hanging around so you could "feel" its presence. Sonia believed the spirit wanted her to leave. We concluded that it had to be a woman who resented another woman taking over her kitchen and bedroom, as any woman would.

One evening as Sonia was returning home from work exhausted, the spirit did something it had not done before–it met her at the door. Terrified, Sonia yelled for it to get out. It did not work. I suggested that perhaps she should take a different tack and try to summon the courage to ask the spirit what she wanted. Have a chat. *All a woman wants sometime is attention, a conversation, someone to communicate with, someone to listen to her.*

Sonia said, "Sure you're right. Where's the for sale sign?" Her fear was understandable, but sometimes picking up and moving is not practical. Her life did not appear to be in danger unless you consider the possibility of literally being scared to death. She figured she would try to last a year until her daughter graduated from high school, and then move. But nearly five years later she still lives there, somehow, having made peace with the ghostly occupant. Both decided they had a right to be there.

*"Home is any four walls that
enclose the right person."*

– Helen Rowland,
"Reflections of a Bachelor Girl" (1909)

eight.
haunted homemaker

Sarah Winchester had a need for a ghost free zone in her home too. She had the means and took a more expensive, if not irrational approach than Sonia. The daughter-in-law of the creator and manufacturer of the Winchester repeater rifle spent 40 years and $5 million building a maze of rooms for the purpose of warding off the curse of vengeful spirits and to assure she would live forever.

Sarah appeared to be a chronically unhappy woman. Her daughter died as a toddler and years later, her husband, George passed away. Unable to recover from their deaths, Sarah sought the advice of a medium, hoping to make a change in her misfortunes.

The medium told her that along with the $20 million her husband left her, she had inherited a huge spiritual debt and was being punished by the spirits of people who had been killed by the Winchester rifle. She was told if she wanted to appease the spirits, lift the curse and live forever she had to give up her residence in

Boston, move out west and buy a house in which she should never stop building.

She moved to San Jose, California and bought an eight room house. Without even a passing acquaintance with architecture or design, Sarah hired carpenters and set out building rooms day and night. She kept that up for 38 years. When she died in 1922, the house had expanded to 160 rooms that featured a trio of elevators, secret passageways, trap doors and stairways, to nowhere, in total violation of the principles of Feng Shui. An intense cleansing of her Boston digs would have been a lot cheaper.

when a woman takes an axe...

HARD HATS

We think our fulfillment comes from other people and in the process we lose ourselves. Not that the other person takes anything from us, but because we choose to leave some of ourselves somewhere else."

— Yvonne Fisher

one.
getting to a sure wall

Yvonne Fisher's only child was her full time project. Everything else simply had to take a back seat. Mothers do that with their first–and only–borns and don't let that child be a male child. You can count on Mom to inspect every breeze to assure it is not blowing harm his way. African American moms, particularly those who are single as Yvonne was then, take raising their baby boys *'real' seriously.* "Giving him an opportunity to survive was more important than anything, " she said.

With her priorities set, Yvonne focused her attention on her son's development for twenty-one years. Her plan was to give him an even chance in a society that can be harsh on black males who take a wrong turn. Her job as administrator with the local government's state's attorney's office made her especially sensitive to young black men. It exposed her to a juvenile and criminal docket that reflected the dim futures of thousands of young men. "I wanted to know that my son could stand on his own and thrive in the level of competition that is out there today," she said.

Yvonne bought a house for them to live in, paid for his education in private school, kept him active in extracurricular activities and saw him through successful years of college and graduate school. Throughout, Yvonne kept herself on hold, although she did not see it that way. In her mind, what she was doing for her son was not a sacrifice, but an essential requirement of parenthood.

To keep her costs down, she did many of her own home repairs and decorating projects. She found the work therapeutic and a window into herself. But it was not until her son was an adult living on his own, that Yvonne fully turned her attention to projects in the house she had lived in for more than twenty years.

She would give the place a makeover. This makeover idea was nothing new, it was merely a resumption of a renovation project she began years before. She stopped when she felt the money she needed for the project was competing with things she wanted to do for her son. More than a pick up of a job once dropped, revisiting the project was a continuation of a personal excavation.

Years earlier, Yvonne had gotten a little peek at another Yvonne. The house work had uncovered a portion of her real self, though not all of her became apparent at once, and she did little to build upon what she discovered. The home remodeling journey had begun in the dining room and there it resumed where Yvonne stripped away the wall covering. It was laborious. But she didn't really mind. She scraped and peeled, eventually removing five layers of wallpaper and two layers of paint before reaching the bare wall.

Certainly, there were days when the work was exhausting and Yvonne was ready to quit and hire someone to finish the job. But after a good night's rest she got up each morning renewed.

"Stripping wallpaper is a very solitary job," Yvonne recalled. "In that solitude, I had a lot of reflective time to talk to myself and look inward. I opened up areas of myself I did not want to look at."

One of those areas was fear. Like many women who have the full time, single responsibility for raising their children, Yvonne was fearful of taking too much time and resources away from her son. She viewed house projects as an unnecessary drain on the cash resources and would forego, them even though she had not investigated the cost nor the work involved in some of the repairs and decorative changes she might have made. "I had tuition to pay," she said.

"That is what handicaps many of us. You look at the job and see enormity and say 'I can't do that.' You make excuses for yourself." Once she took on the projects she had put off for years, Yvonne realized they were not only inexpensive, but she could do much of it herself. "I wish I realized years ago that I could do this."

The wallpaper project was a rebirth. "It was like stripping away the old veneer and releasing what was underneath." What was underneath was very nice strong plaster walls in the century old house. "I felt tremendously good once I got all of the paper off."

The experience allows you to reach your own psychological foundation. For Yvonne, finally seeing the bare walls of the house was like seeing herself unfolded. "You've removed that shell, that covering and your inner strength comes through."

While undertaking her project, Yvonne found within herself someone she suspected was always there, a much surer personality than the one she had been most of her life. She allowed raising her son to distract her from her own need for self work. "I got lost in the process of parenting. And in some ways that detracted from relationships because I did not work at them the way I worked at raising my child or even the way I worked at removing the wallpaper."

Yvonne came from a strong household with parents who were married fifty-one years. Her father taught her to be independent. But there is a lot of competition for a young person's attention as they seek fulfillment through others even though they know better. "I was as independent as anybody growing up but once involved in a relationship, that changed," Yvonne says recalling her romance with her former husband. "A lot of times we abandon the very strengths we need to survive in a relationship. We mold ourselves into what the other person desires from us. It took me a while to get back."

The stripped wallpaper filled six, twenty gallon plastic trash bags. For Yvonne, the bags contained more than old wall covering. They held the remnants of her emotional and psychological excavation. "Everything happens to us as a learning experience, negative or positive, and you have to draw from it and leave the garbage behind," Yvonne says. "Now I can sit down and look at what I really want to do in this house: Fix it up and move."

when a woman takes an axe...

*"All women love to get flowers. I love flowers.
But if you really want to get to my heart bring me an
electric screw gun.
Bring me an electric sander."*

– Sarah E. Holley

two.
a knight in shining armor

No matter how independent, women still turn a trusting heart to men when it comes to heavy lifting, mechanical problems or answers to the unknown. And it amuses me that we accept their representations without question whether or not those answers are supported by expertise or prior knowledge. I suspect what is at play is an emotional need on our part for trust and rescue that develops in girlhood and becomes an intuitive part of how we relate in the world.

A notable consequence of this *Knight in Shining Armor Syndrome*, as I call it, is a woman's failure to trust her own judgment. A woman's judgment, her intuition, is an important element of her unique makeup. It should not be compromised.

A story about wood floors that Sarah Holley tells illustrates the point. Sarah bought a twenty-one room mansion in Baltimore's historic Bolton Hill in the 1990's. The 7,200 square foot building was a

19th century, four-story Victorian with terrific curb appeal. However, inside was nothing like outside. *It was a mess.* It had been sliced into nine efficiency apartments and no one had lived there for seven years. Trash was piled up throughout, ceilings were falling, radiators were cracked, no electricity, and the wood floors were in bad shape.

Yet, Sarah was undaunted. "The first thing I did was picture the house the way I wanted it," she said. "I saw an opportunity to transform something." With the help of hired hands and an electrician, she got a lot of work done. Still, it was nearly a year before she did anything about the wood floors. Restoration involved sanding the surfaces and sealing them with a polyurethane coating.

The electric sanding machine she needed was big and heavy and powered with air pressure that helped it move smoothly across the floor. For the novice user, the machine could easily get away and create gouges in a floor if allowed to linger in one spot. Though she had never sanded floors before, Sarah planned from the start to sand them herself. However she allowed herself to be frightened out of doing it. Male friends told her she would ruin the floors.

"They said using the sanding machines required expertise," she recalled. "They told me I didn't know what I was doing and I would ruin the floors with gouges." Sarah had a small budget that did not include replacing the floors or hiring a professional floor restoration company. A mistake could be costly. "I believed them. So I didn't do the floors."

She said although her friends' discouragement irritated her, she never thought it had colored her can-do attitude until she watched a certain television program. "I saw a woman on a home repair show sand floors," Sarah said. "It was easy. The machine did all the work. The woman just walked behind it." The demonstration made Sarah angry with herself. "It really bothered me after I watched this woman just walk behind that machine and do those floors. I had been thinking I was going to put gouges in the floors. All that time, I could have done it myself."

The following week, Sarah rented a sanding machine and edger and got to work on her floors and the wood steps. "The outcome was perfect," she said. Putting other voices above her own prevented Sarah from taking a chance on herself. "I could have sanded the floors if I had not listened to them," she said. Of course, *the error was not in listening to her male friends but in not listening to herself.*

"When I work, I'm in rain, I'm in snow, I'm in mud–and I'm color coordinated."

– Alice E. Burley,
construction site supervisor

three.
a man's world

It takes a strong, wily mind to navigate a successful career in the male-dominated world of the building trades and construction. Now, here's a spot where control is the operative word. If you think these snug little enclaves are tough places for a man to be then enter as a woman dressed up in chinos, steel toed boots, checkered shirt, lipstick and a hard hat. Everybody gets confused. Embedded in crevices of these uniquely difficult labor-intensive, high-paying, season-fickle jobs is the male ego. The ego-investment is in the rule of control and domination under which men in these jobs tend to operate whether they are relating solely among themselves or in mixed company. The players do not easily adjust to difference. It is a man's world and if a woman is in it you can bet she has figured the natives out and earned her place.

Everything a woman knows and feels about being a woman must be left outside the job site gate, say the women who work on the other side. The construction site is no place for feelings. It is straight, linear thinking and task oriented, the one place where all that counts is the process and learning how men function. You don't have to become one of them, just understand the territory, says Alice Harrington a general contractor whose company, Palace Designs, does building renovations in the Washington, D.C. area.

"I tried being one of the boys," Alice says. But it took a few hard lessons for her to learn "I am not. You may be the boss, but they still try to count your money for you." To maintain perspective for both sides, Alice says she did something as subtle as keeping her fingernails manicured "just to remind me I am a lady and remind them I am a lady."

A woman's presence in a man's world serves to highlight the distinct differences between the feminine and male way of processing information and relating to the world. *The two sexes differ in more than the obviousness of their plumbing.* Their wiring is completely different. You could say a man's electrical wires run horizontally or vertically, never crossing. That's what allows them their riveted, horse blinders ability to focus step by step and stay in one task no matter what else is happening around them.

On the other hand, women's wiring is more like a web. Women are contextual. They like to stroll the mall, throwing out a net to pull in all the options around them for consideration. Anthropologist Helen Fisher describes this distinctive behavior as "Web thinking versus step thinking; an emphasis on the whole versus a focus on the parts; multitasking versus doing one thing at a time." She notes that there is nothing wrong with either. They're just different and it is a difference that is critical knowledge for the woman who must operate in a man's world.

when a woman takes an axe...

The men know exactly what each other is thinking and on the job they are making a point among themselves, Alice says. "It's all about control that comes out of their fear and ignorance" of the female who is in his space and out of context. The woman who ventures in must know the rules going in, be a quick study if she doesn't or be prepared for a short career.

Alice Burley learned fast. If you played the game *What's My Line?* with her as a panelist you'd never guess her to be a construction worker. Her high cheek bones, flawless brown skin, long black hair, pursed lips and petite 5'4" height are the look that draws the stereotypical construction site wolf calls and whistles. But as a construction site supervisor all Alice wants and commands is respect.

"As a woman, I cannot play with them or go in soft. I have to go in serious. Otherwise they play with you."

Alice attended night school for eight years to earn a master's degree in architecture. But it was a field trip to a roof under construction that made her fall in love with building. "Just seeing how it was put together and the difference between what we draw as architects and how it works in reality was an eye opener."

She shifted her focus and developed a career in which she has worked as a project manager and site inspector and supervisor on school construction projects in Maryland. At work, Alice is the boss and often is the only female around. But the name on her hard hat and the signature on her field reports don't say "Alice"–for a reason.

Her job as site supervisor requires her to produce field reports to record any job or procedure that needs to be corrected. The architect gets the reports and uses them to oversee corrections by the contractor.

Alice says when she first got started she signed her full name on the reports. However, "No one would do the work," she said and she wasn't sure why. After a while she figured she'd try something. To see if it would make a difference, Alice changed her signature and signed all documents as A.E. Burley. It seemed to work. "As long as I was signing the reports A.E. Burley, everything was getting done."

Although the men addressed her as Miss Burley in meetings they didn't make the connection with the A.E. Burley who signed the reports, she said. "I would show up on the site anytime of the day or night and start directing work and making my reports." After a while the men caught on. "And they started taking me seriously."

Alice learned that a woman in a male dominated venue must have a personal standard and stick to her word. It is a critical lesson that teaches you how to live with yourself and provides assurances for others. She recalled an incident in which applying her standards clashed with one worker but protected the others and made an important point in her favor. "I had to remove a guy from one of my sites one time. He cussed out one of the men over a misplaced tool. I told my site foreman the guy needed to be removed by the next day." When she returned a few days later, the man was still there.

She had to stand her ground. Alice sent a message to the worker's supervisor that if he showed up again he would be considered trespassing and arrested. She was firm and made it clear she was prepared to follow through. He got the message and never returned. "He was bad for morale and I cannot tolerate bad attitudes on the site."

Working with male contractors, Alice noticed distinct differences in how she and the men perform on the job. For one, "Men make deals," she said. "I don't make deals because they can compromise a job with shoddy material and work." Another distinction is men act

when a woman takes an axe...

as if they know everything, she said. "When I don't know something I will ask. I've learned there is no harm in saying I don't know. And in the construction industry you won't know everything."

As project manager, Alice must have a knowledge base that's broad and deep. She has learned types of soils, the kind of masonry needed on the job and the details of the installation for the electrical and plumbing systems. Once a woman with a reserved manner, she has learned to speak up and voice her opinion personally and professionally. She would like to see more women in the field, but has met only a handful who were electricians and masons. Her theory is it is not the trade that keeps women out. "It's the women who think they cannot do it," she said. "There's no reason not to try." Most times women can do a better job simply because we take our time and don't have an investment of ego.

"I was blessed to see something prettier than what it was."

– Dolores Ellis

four.
gifted eye

New construction has no appeal to Dolores Ellis and Charleene Doverspike, two visionary women living and working in cities separated by 400 miles–one in Savannah, the other in Baltimore. They had never met. Though lineage and skin-tone would belie the fact, these sisters in the mortar are identical twins in their knack for loving houses back to life. Give them an old house at its worst and they thrill at the challenge of breathing in new energy where energy was declared gone.

A dark, dilapidated rowhouse with its second-floor bathroom collapsing off its rear may seem a sure candidate for the wrecking ball to most. But to Ellis and Doverspike this is a gem that needs a loving touch. They are women with a gifted eye, that crystal, intuitive, part of the mind which sees potential few others can picture. They see beauty in impossibly unattractive structures, whether it is a rowhouse or an abandoned mini estate with overgrown grounds and its innards stripped to the beams.

Their gifted eye beholds a home renewed, freshly painted and brilliant with sunlight pouring through new skylights and transoms. Cascading stairwells, pocket doors, hardwood floors, graceful archways and built-in cabinetry accent the transformation in their minds.

Neither woman has any formal training in architecture, design or any of the building trades. Yet they are architectural visionaries who can see the broadest of possibilities in houses no one else wants.

It is not farfetched to think that every woman has a third eye, a natural intuition that we all possess but don't exercise enough. Call it the visual side of intuition that feels and sees the good potential in all things, whether it is a derelict building or a wayward child. Where others of us second guess ourselves out of really good ideas, Charleene and Mrs. Ellis, as she prefers to be addressed, learned to trust their judgment and instinct for design and what they liked. As a consequence, their vision, their gifted eye, is sharply developed much like a muscle that's constantly worked. For Charleene and Mrs. Ellis, following their vision was not a question.

— ~ —

The house on West Hall Street in Savannah captured Mrs. Ellis' heart and imagination on first sight during a tour of the city in 1989. It was a little Victorian estate with a three-story main house improved by balconies and porches and accompanied by its own carriage house. The appearance of the 110 year old property harkened back to the days of excess and full-body corsets. But unoccupied for twenty-five years the place had fallen on hard times.

The grounds were overgrown and trash was piled up. In the twilight, the backyard was a bawdy house where neighborhood prostitutes worked an adjacent street servicing their johns. Inside the main house, the sky was visible from at least four locations on the first floor. It had been stripped of everything of value – marble fireplaces, brass sconces, chandeliers, doorknobs, even the staircases. It appeared there was nothing left to do but tap it with a bulldozer and put it out of its misery.

The first time she saw the place, Mrs. Ellis told herself she was looking at a grand old lady someone has tried to kill. "I fell in love with it and knew from the start I could do something with it," she recalled. She had owned seventeen houses from Washington, D.C. to San Francisco at one time or another, but she'd never undertaken a renovation before. She decided on the spot this would be her first. Months later, she bought the dowager property for $45,000 and set out to rescue it from the scourges of time and neglect.

Inspecting the century-old Victorian house was an adventure. The staircases had been stolen away so a ladder was needed to reach the upper floors. Once up there "you could see all the way to the basement," she recalled. "But there was a kindred spirit there and I could see the beauty of the place."

She commenced the arduous restoration project in 1990 and for more than a year lived in a nearby motel while she renovated the carriage house. She was not only bringing a house back to use but inspiring a neighborhood, whose residents were taken with the energetic African American woman, and pitched in to help. With the helping hands of her new-found friends she dug out dirt from the basement, hauled away trash from the grounds and undertook a host of other tasks. She hired plumbers, electricians and carpenters for major infrastructure work but did much of the hard detail work herself, stripping woodwork and redoing doors.

The carriage house was restored first. Mrs. Ellis moved in, living there for two years while undertaking the restoration of the main house, which called for complete reconstruction and tracking down period pieces to make the house as authentic as it once was. On that score she had a little unexpected help late one night when she was heading to bed in the attic, which was the first area of the main house she completed. Someone from this world or perhaps the next, but clearly someone, visited her with instructions to "Go to the first bedroom at the top of the stairs and look in the closet on the left hand side," Mrs. Ellis recalled. "There's a piece of marble that goes on your mantelpiece."

Mrs. Ellis said she was not afraid. "I just said OK, how are you doin?" When she followed the direction she had been given and checked the closet, she found a long, beautiful piece of marble.

Patience had to be an important tool on Mrs. Ellis' workbench. It took six labor-intensive years and a total investment of $400,000 to complete the house. In September 1997, the elegantly restored mansion with its four guest bedrooms, verandas, private garden and carriage house was opened for business as a bed and breakfast with luxurious accommodations.

The carriage house served as the Honeymoon Cottage with a kitchen, washer and dryer, living area, a half bath on the first floor, a loft bedroom with queen size bed, full bath and small roof deck. Mrs. Ellis christened the estate the "The Grande Toots Inn," in honor of the childhood nickname she was given by an older brother who called her "Toots." It is a wonderful sight in a city that is making a remarkable comeback, in part thanks to a visionary renovator who "was blessed to see something prettier than what it was."

The Grand Toots Inn operates today under another name, Georgetown Inn, and another proprietor.

"The universe definitely supports you if you are willing to take the first step. The power is in saying 'I'm going to do it' and then committing to doing it and realizing that your words really have power."

– Charleene Doverspike

five.
good bones

The flight to the suburbs that began in the 1970's devastated neighborhoods and left a staggering inventory of abandoned and boarded up properties in scores of cities. Philadelphia has 27,746, Baltimore more than 11,000, Houston 8,000, Kansas City 5,000 and Los Angeles more than 1,800. These are just a sampling. There are many more. Thus far, solutions to the blight have challenged both officials and the private sector. The only remedy may be in a magic wand or in cloning Charleene Doverspike a couple thousand times.

More than fifty of Charleene's rejuvenated rowhouses dot the urban landscape between Washington and Baltimore. Some of the houses are no more than 10 feet wide and in them all, she saw something to be rescued. She saw "good bones." In Canton, an up and coming, pricey community in southeast Baltimore that rings the east Harbor, Charleene's *Elegant City Homes* renovation company set the tone for how to create charm and luxury in a house only 10 feet wide.

To Charleene a house with "good bones" is one with a well thought out layout and rooms that flow one to another. She has taken modest old houses and given them zest with custom built-ins, tongue and groove oak flooring, bulkheads, skylights, transoms and accent lights. She added something none of these homes ever had before–plenty of sunlight and a powder room on the first floor.

Looking at her handiwork you would think that this thoughtful woman with the bright blonde ponytail and radiant smile has extensive formal training in architecture, carpentry or design, but she does not. Charleene's background is economics and finance, two areas that eventually bored her silly, she said. She earned a degree in finance attending night school at Mercy University in Georgia while working as a bank teller during the day. But as it turned out, "It was not for me," she said.

Until 1988, Charleene was uncertain what exactly was for her. A crumbling marriage and unfulfilling career backed her into life as a home renovator. It's a life which has earned her notice and respect among tradesmen and homebuyers over the years.

She was living in Washington, D.C. with her husband and their five year old son, Jason. Home was a four-bedroom rental house with skylights that leaked. Her income of $21,000 was all the family had coming in. To pay the $700 monthly rent, Charleene sublet the best three of their four bedrooms. A mother and child were in one, and two couples occupied the other two rooms.

The dormitory-like living provided no privacy ever. And what really got to her was the water pouring into the kitchen through the three skylights that leaked every time it rained. "I was embarrassed to tell my parents how I was living," Charleene said. "If my mom had known I had all these people living there to pay my rent it would have killed her."

When Charleene decided that something had to shift, she had every pot she owned set up around the kitchen to catch water. The landlord wouldn't repair the leaks. The portion of the house Charleene and her family lived in was an add-on with no heat. Ice formed on the inside of the windows and they burned wood in a fireplace to keep warm. Everyday, the family awoke with sore throats. One day she decided to buy a house, a seemingly implausible decision considering her finances. "I decided God didn't put me on this earth to live like that."

Certainly, Charleene didn't always live like that. She and her husband were entrepreneurs who owned a couple of fitness centers where the couple trained bodybuilders and promoted fitness contests. They were enterprising and fearless. What they knew about running the business they learned while they were in it. Life was good until the bottom fell out of the fitness industry and the business ended in bankruptcy.

Her husband, a writer and martial arts master, was out of work for three years. She was getting low paying jobs. The lack of finances strained their marriage and brought it to an end. "It was a hard life and everyday you felt like you were someplace you weren't supposed to be."

With a bankruptcy and family income of only $21,000 a year Charleene believed "I really didn't have anything going for me that would tell me I could buy a house." Still, she decided she was going to buy one anyway.

She found a house listed in the newspaper under investment properties in a neighborhood she liked and went to take a look. It was a rowhouse. "What struck me about it was it was made of brick, so I figured it wouldn't be eaten up with termites or blown down. And it was small enough that I could envision I could handle it."

She made the call to the investors. They were two guys whose only deal was making money, she said. "I told them right up front that I didn't have a dime. But I guess they heard something in my voice that convinced them I was really committed to doing this."

The investors helped her. The arrangement resulted in a monthly mortgage payment of $761, a few dollars more than she was paying in rent. She bought the house without seeing the inside, taking the owners' word that the plumbing and the electrical worked. "I gave them $1 and we signed a contract."

"I always trust people," Charleene said. "If you got to go through life thinking that you can't believe people, what's the point of being on earth? It's not a fun way to live." Inside, the old plaster walls had huge cracks and broken lathe. The kitchen and bathroom were in shambles, paint was peeling from the walls and around the windows. This was not a disaster to Charleene, nor were the rats' nests under the radiators.

She threw herself into the house, going by after work and on weekends. She spent the first three weeks cleaning and tearing out dilapidated kitchen cabinets. "It never occurred to me to be scared. I just thought that house had a lot of bad wrinkles. I thought I could fix it. I didn't know why. I didn't know how to do it." To school herself she bought books, magazines and studied pictures. "I'm somebody who the harder my life gets the more resilient I become. I guess it's because I'm hardheaded."

For five months, Charleene worked on the house by herself. One day a man who was looking to buy in the neighborhood saw her working on her place and asked her advice. In the exchange of information, she learned he was a physicist who knew plumbing. She helped him choose a house and they agreed to a partnership in which he provided the capital and muscle to help fix up her house and she helped him with his.

With tile she saved from the fitness center, Charleene covered the kitchen floor in a mosaic of white, gray, red and pink. "I had all different colors but I had tile on the floor," she says laughing at the memory. With $7,000 invested by her new partner she bought kitchen appliances and supplies for a counter top she helped make.

With that house, Charleene's enterprising self as a home renovator took shape. She started feeling brave and empowered. She got together with friends and bought one house after another which they renovated, uses her design ideas, and then sold. Tray ceilings, skylights, transoms, built-ins and cozy kitchen features became Charleene's signature in her Elegant City Homes.

Renovation can be an expensive affair with cost overruns a given. Charleene saved on some of these costs by moving into a house while under renovation then moving on once it was sold. She used the proceeds to buy the next one and continue the cycle, seldom living in a house more than a year. By 2001 she had a portfolio of more than fifty houses she had renovated and often sold before the project was completed.

Thinking back on the early days, Charleene assessed the events that made her successful and concluded that what worked for her can work for anyone. "Every time you take an action to make your life different and you tell yourself you need to take an action," she says, "the things you need to happen start showing up for you. It seems that's all it ever takes."

when a woman takes an axe...

"There are serious consequences to shortcuts."

– *Jocelyn Garlington*

six.
an extraordinary gift

Jocelyn Garlington lived a happy, carefree life as a renter most of her adult life. Then she lost her job and had to move back home to her parents' house in the old neighborhood. "It was not my plan to live in the neighborhood," she said. She loved downtown life and would miss it.

Back home, the people next door were Swedish immigrants, the Olsens. Mrs. Olsen was a homemaker and her husband was a retired engineer from Westinghouse. The Olsens were not just neighbors but best friends with Jocelyn's parents. They looked out for each other and did things together. In a neighborhood distinctive in its racial homogeneity, the Olsens stood out.

Returning home as an adult was difficult for Jocelyn. Like many parents, hers seemed to be stuck in a time warp when it came to her. She was in her late 30's and missed living on her own. And her father was dying. The emotional and psychological demands–spoken and unspoken–were great. All Jocelyn knew was she was back in her childhood house but truly could not 'go home again.' Still, there she was back in the house, back in the neighborhood.

Mr. Olsen came to her rescue. He invited her to live in the second floor apartment of his house next door, a little deal he worked out in advance in a quiet conversation with her father. In preparation for her move in, Mr. Olsen painted and changed wallpaper. He included her on trips to pick out the kind of paper she wanted. Mr. Olsen was a lucky gambler so the house was meticulously cared for, financed with money he won at the track. Whoever lived there had to be compatible because there were no locks on the doors

Life in the house was satisfying for her. She and the Olsens lived like housemates rather than tenant and landlord. He would send the newspaper up to her everyday after he'd read it. They never knocked, they just opened the door and let themselves in, like family. After Mrs. Olsen's death and as Mr. Olsen aged, becoming ill, Jocelyn took over care of the house. She shopped for him, took out the trash and cleaned up. Mr. Olsen told Jocelyn's family he wanted to leave her the 75 year old, thirteen-room house. When he died, the promise was kept. The place was no palace. Termites had eaten through the load bearing beams and scores of repairs were needed.

Jocelyn thought about selling the property. "It became a mausoleum to me. Mrs. Olsen died there, Mr. Olsen was dead, Dad died. I really wanted to leave because it was really burdensome." But she kept thinking about what a wonderful gift it was. *You don't just part with such an extraordinary gift.* "There was a quality about the house, the spirit of the gift and the familiarity and the comfort that I felt here, that even though it was really hard sometimes, I couldn't put it on the market. It was an extraordinary gift." Jocelyn let the idea of

when a woman takes an axe...

selling drift from her mind even though "There were people always telling me to get rid of it. It was almost as if they didn't think I should have it."

One particularly cold winter she began to wonder about her decision. "I had so little money." It was difficult to heat thirteen rooms in a house with so many windows. "It was so cold in here. You could see your own breath." Still she stayed and called on a long-time friend who was a contractor to do some work in the house. After he painted a few rooms, she found she couldn't even count on friends she thought had talent.

"He did not do a good job," Jocelyn noted. He painted windows shut and the paint started peeling two years later. "I had no significant other and I had no money. Hiring help was a problem. They were unreliable. That made me realize even more I had to learn to do things myself. It's amazing to me how many men don't know about home repair. I use to think *just call a man*."

Gradually, the house and her mother's house next door defined Jocelyn's lifestyle. They both needed work. She had learned enough about electricity and plumbing from her father not to be afraid. As a child, The Hechinger's home supply store was a favorite outing with her father when he was in search of washers and fittings. Jocelyn installed her own air conditioners and replaced the plastic air stoppers when necessary.

"It's all consuming. When I'm not in the yard I'm thinking about being in the yard. When I'm not painting, I'm thinking about painting. In every room of my house I have a bucket with a scraper and some joint compound. I find myself always scraping and fixing. I read a lot of magazines on home repair." *Readers Digest Encyclopedia of Home Repairs* was a favorite and she watched all the public television home shows. "I've got pipes and I've got toilet seats that need replacing that are leaning up against the wall."

Jocelyn took notice of how some men are always tinkering, like her father and Mr. Olsen used to do. "There is something addictive about this activity. Dad and Sven used to stand by the gate and gaze, taking notice of the sagging gutters–which they would repair–or the buckle in the pavement, taking care of things, pruning the trees. I find myself doing the same thing."

In leaving her a real estate legacy, "Mr. Olsen gave me survival skills," Jocelyn says. "It's amazing the stuff that comes back to me that I remember him doing. It is my sanctuary. Mr. Olsen let me stay somewhere where I got comfortable."

For Jocelyn there also are direct benefits to homeown*her*ship that fall on the personal asset side of the ledger. She noticed she had become a more observant, careful, efficient and stronger person than when she was a renter. Along with ownership came a feeling of control and responsibility that engaged a side of the personality that is not otherwise activated. And that's wonderful. "As a renter you called your landlord. As an owner I'm capable of planning and I am thoughtful."

She also wanted to know what makes things work. "I've become a deconstructionalist." she says. There was a time when an appliance that stopped working well became a donation to Good Will. "Now I fix everything. I don't buy anything new. If I can't fix it, I take it somewhere and they have to pronounce it dead. I don't just put stuff in a box and give it away."

She has rewired lamps, fixed the toaster and taken apart the VCR to give it a cleaning with alcohol. "Not that I am so strapped for funds that I couldn't buy another VCR but I respect the construction of

when a woman takes an axe...

things and how they are and I'm not intimidated anymore." Another lesson learned was the importance of not skipping steps. "I used to be impatient with the rules governing preliminaries. But with a home if I do shortcuts I could kill myself. I can't put a light fixture up without turning the power off. I need to turn the water off before working on the sink. There are serious consequences to shortcuts."

Other lessons brought about by the extraordinary gift of home-own*her*ship Mr. Olsen bequeathed to Jocelyn reached right into her purse in an unexpected way. "I used to have a Voodoo economics policy about my checkbook. If I didn't get an overdraft notice it was cool. Now I actually write down my debit transactions and things I was careless about before I became a homeowner, I anticipate."

"We assume because we are told we can't, we can't."

– Sarah Holley

seven.
one bite at a time

Renovating a house has a romantic, adventurous appeal when you're talking about it. At that point, visions of the finished project in all its splendiferous detail dominates the picture frame of the mind. But working through the details contained in that zone known as the *in between* can feel overwhelming as you attempt to bring the art to life. There are days when you wonder how you could have thought you could do a home renovation project yourself when the closest you ever came to one was the time you painted the hallway.

Sarah Holley experienced moments like that as she went about renovating her mansion. They were psychologically and emotionally challenging moments. Restoring the twenty-one room mansion she bought in an historic district in Baltimore was filled with nothing if not details. Starting was simple enough but hanging in there was really hard. To stay mentally fresh for the work, she did what many urban renovators do and adopted a few psychological tricks. She applied a popular maxim that advises "The only way to eat an elephant is one bite at a time." She then created a "little successes" approach to get through.

Little successes can be thought of as dining in a Tapas restaurant, gradually eating everything on the menu, one appetizer at a time. It's less daunting than ordering a huge main course all at once. Sarah began by telling herself "There was no hurry. I didn't have a deadline. I could learn and make mistakes." Then she'd do just the tasks she felt like doing a little at a time.

With big projects you get to a point where you have a psychological need to see items crossed off the list. To create a feeling of accomplishment, Sarah did tasks out of sequence. Logically, the first step after hauling out the trash that had built up would have been to hire an electrician to establish power in the house. Finding one was a chore, so instead Sarah bought wall sconces, decorative accessories and picked out paint colors and tile patterns. "I did that to keep me going. Instead of tackling the major things in the house I went for the cosmetic."

Instead of getting the walls and moldings scraped and painted, she focused on how great pocket doors would look. She realized that when there are a multitude of jobs to do, handle the ones you like first, even if they are only cosmetic. "You can accomplish more when you feel you are getting somewhere."

Now, of course, there is a downside to that approach if the strategy is based on emotion absent of logic. For instance, Sarah continued to put off getting the electricity installed. Instead she searched for a plumber to put in a new furnace. Less than 24 hours after the furnace was installed someone broke into the house and stole all of the copper pipes from the furnace. "They just sawed the pipes off."

Had she installed electricity first, she could have put in an alarm system that might have prevented the theft. She also lost the antique mirror she had painstakingly paid for over a year on layaway in an antique shop. Fortunately, the mirror thief was a few bricks short of a load; he sold it back to the same antique shop using his correct identification and she was able to recover it. The copper thief got away clean.

Another potential problem started at the beginning. Getting the house in shape meant Sarah had to please the neighborhood association and the historical society who had rules and covenants she had to abide by. Their demands ranged from the occupancy of the house to the colors she could paint it on the outside. That's how it is when you buy a house in an area with an historic designation.

Sarah wanted to have tenants to help offset the monthly mortgage payment. The society wanted the mansion reestablished as a single-family home, which may have worked in the 19th century when people slept in their coats and fireplaces were the sole source of heat. But in the 20th century that was fiscally illogical in the face of one month's heating bill.

Any renovations Sarah planned for the building's façade required that she submit her written plans for approval by the historical society. There were guidelines for cleaning the brick—no chemicals, sandblasting only. If she was going to paint the doors and window frames she had to choose her colors from a list of designated colors the society kept. "Suppose I didn't like any of the colors on the list? I had already bought the house. It can really be frightening when you are standing alone and you want to fix your house the way you want to and there are these people," Sarah said.

Rather than fight them, Sarah did the smart thing and joined the organization, becoming an active voice. Many meetings and a few compromises later Sarah was able to proceed with the plans for her house. It would not be the single-family home the neighborhood association wanted. Sarah would have her tenants but she would not reestablish the mansion as the dense rooming house it had been–it was a good compromise.

What is really lasting is not the paint job
but the painting lessons.

eight.
courage takes practice

Women are by nature empathetic souls and society's peacemakers. We can feel someone else's pain. We want to kiss the bruise and make it all better. It is a disposition that often finds a woman settling for something she did not want in order to avoid conflict and protect a male ego. That behavior may work in social and familial situations but often is no good in business. And hiring a contractor to do work at your house is business.

Any woman who has ever paid for a job that was not done to her satisfaction but she accepted for fear of "offending" or "bothering" the contractor and or it seemed too late and too much trouble to make him redo it, can relate and will love LaTanya Richardson and Dianna Brochendorff.

LaTanya wanted a brick patio in the rear of her spacious Tudor house in Encino, California. She knew exactly the kind of brick she wanted and provided the contractor a sample to assure that she got what she had in mind. The red brick had unique properties and was not easy to find in the usual retail home improvement stores in the area but it was available with a little effort. The job was scheduled for a day she expected to be away but she left confident it would be done according to her specifications and looked forward to the finished project.

The contractor followed through. By the time LaTanya returned home he had finished laying the brick patio that covered about 1/4 acre of terraced slopes and broad steps. There was one problem. It was the wrong brick.

This took me back to my own experiences. Imagine how annoyed you would feel seeing the job completed and beautiful in every way except it is not what you asked for. It has happened to me more than once. The irritation of an unpainted wood fence with squared off handrails surrounding my porch. It was not what I had discussed with the architect/carpenter I hired. The work not only clashed with the Victorian style house but was insecurely installed.

After voicing a weak, unconvincing objection, I paid the architect off figuring I would get someone else to fix the job. That was ridiculous. I was the one with the leverage. I had the check but I gave away my power because I had been thoroughly conditioned to be accommodating and avoid conflict. I didn't have the nerve to tell the contractor the job was unsatisfactory and not what we agreed on. Since the work was already finished I felt it was too late. I didn't want to have him redo it and make him mad at me. I wanted to be agreeable and liked.

And, he was counting on that. Most all of them are. Unless otherwise conditioned, it is natural to do what is convenient *which to a contractor often means using cheaper, inferior material and taking shortcuts.*

when a woman takes an axe...

This is not to paint a picture of bad people. It is a picture of real people who yield to genuine human weakness and are practiced in the art of getting away with something. And women aid and abet the behavior because we don't want any trouble. The male folks we hire count on that because that's the rewarding behavior they learned in interacting with their womenfolk. Each time we let a contractor get away with a bad job we reinforce their bad practices.

So you end up with a cheap grade of indoor paint on an outdoor project, inappropriate, improperly installed handrails and instead of screws to lock down the flooring of your wood deck you get nails that loosen in groups until all their heads pop up before the deck season is over—*I'm really not bitter.* You also get the wrong color brick.

Well, if LaTanya's contractor had any bad practices—she, who is also the wife of actor Samuel L. Jackson, and an accomplished actor and director herself—broke the cycle. The brick was laid and set in cement but it didn't matter to LaTanya, who played the role of *Atallah "Queenie" Sims*, a tough judge on A&E's weekly television series, *100 Centre Street.* If you're not quite sure just how tough Judge Sims is, you find out from the pet line she delivers to a hapless three-time loser "Your parole officer hasn't been born yet." If you're not quite certain how tough LaTanya, the woman and homeowner is, you find out when she tells the bricklayer "Dig it up!"

"It was not what I wanted and he knew it," she said. He said he could not find the brick and thought the one he selected would do. It was just another block of brick to him. But he had to remove it and he knew it if he expected to get paid. LaTanya asserted her will and got what she wanted and what was agreed to from the beginning.

— ~ —

allegra bennett | 95

Dianna Brochendorff thought she had an agreement with the contractor working on the office building she was developing at 18th Street and Connecticut Avenue in Washington, D.C. Dianna had ten years experience in commercial real estate development, an industry she was introduced to by her former husband. She wanted the plumbing in the seven story building wrapped to insulate tenants from the sound of flushing toilets. She memorialized the order in writing.

When she inspected the job the plumbing had not been wrapped. "It was complete disrespect for me even though I was the one paying him," Dianna said. It was a time, material and money situation with union workers being paid a premium. The contractor, doubtlessly, counted on Dianna to accept the job because the walls already had been hung. He was mistaken. "I had them tear up the walls in seven stories and do what I asked to be done - wrap the plumbing," she said. That was a cost the contractor had to eat.

Commit to a bigger game

nine.
going for it

It seems the lesson about fear has to be relearned with each challenge, even by women of considerable achievement. That is a good thing to know. Charleene Doverspike had become accomplished at acquiring and renovating houses over a dozen years but, surprisingly, harbored a fear about asking for money. She had renovated forty-five houses but it was not until the 46th that she applied for a bank loan. She had been afraid all of that time that she would be turned down.

She avoided bank loans by being creative. She lived in a house until renovation was completed. She'd then sell it, buy another and make it just habitable for occupancy, move in, renovate and sell. The cycle worked for her and she didn't have to have a bank mortgage. But the time came when she wanted to do bigger projects than before and she needed financing from a bank. But fear held her back.

"It's what holds us all back. Just our very own fear. I was so afraid to call the bank. I had this bankruptcy. I had all these fears they wouldn't say yes. Why would they say yes? I could give them a hundred reasons not to."

Finally she realized if she were ever going to get the project done she would have to be prepared to accept rejection–she had to at least call. "I'm sure that's what stops all of us in everything that we don't do. We're just afraid of rejection," Charleene said. "If you could just say, 'okay, I'm afraid,' and do it anyway because you always live (survive) and oftentimes you are a lot better. But if you won't go out there and at least take the action to start it, then you'll never know.' She got the loan and another source of fear bit the dust.

FOUNDATION FUNDAMENTALS

——————————— [book three] ———————————

Instead of dealing with faith we try to make logic of faith, which is the confusion."

**– *Anna Maria Horsford,*
*actor***

one.

faith house

Anna Maria Horsford can take silence and turn it into a side splitting platform for laughter. She is also an old hand at homeown**her**ship and can make you laugh *and* cry, in turn, at some of her *Tales From The Landlord*. In 1984, she decided to allow Hollywood to experience her talents and moved out west from her home in Harlem, USA. By that time she had already owned three houses in New York . In each she oversaw the relocation of walls, windows, ceilings and outdoor ponds. But of all the houses she has owned, and or managed for her family, her experience with her home in the Oaks community of Los Feliz transcended bricks and mortar. It was the temple that provided the most profound lesson in faith she had experienced. It is the house that the comedic actor says she "bought with no money." It is the home, her spiritual retreat, that she embraces as "My Faith House."

Anna Maria has done well in her craft, enjoying success in the movies and on series television as both a dramatic and comedic performer. In the 1980's she played Sherman Helmsley's spoiled preacher's daughter, *Thelma*, on the television series, *Amen*. In the new millennium she got another bite at series television entertaining a fresh generation of viewers in the role of *Dee*, a security guard, on *The Wayans Brothers.*

But it hadn't been easy for her. For one awfully challenging year and a half before she landed that role, she endured the dreaded career dry spell. "I was in a work crisis, I could not get a job," Anna Maria says. She owned her house but selling it offered no solution. After the earthquake of 1991, the value of the house had dropped so low that her mortgage was higher than the house was worth.

"I was in such a depression by then," she said. Anna Maria didn't know how long the down turn would last. She felt 'unbankable' and unappreciated. Friends checked in on her, asking how things were going. Although she was candid with them about her situation, they thought the woman with the comic timing was kidding. "Nobody knew."

By 1998, Anna Maria's time in the valley was drawing to a close. The method was amazing and filled with grace. A phenomenal chain of events occurred not because of any savvy ideas Anna Maria thought up but because she put her trust in a higher power and followed instructions. The turning point began with a call from a girlfriend who told Anna Maria of an insistent dream she had the night before. She dreamed she was asked to give Anna Maria a message from God that said "You've gotta let it go." The message didn't say let go of what.

Anna Maria hung up from her friend and pondered the message. As she considered the words of her friend's dream, a thought came to her that was so pointed she spoke it aloud. "You know how some-times you feel something and then you verbalize it and it clicks?" she asked. The provocative thought was "let go of the house."

"I was thinking I don't have a job and I haven't had a job and I probably will never have a job again," she said. She had a large art collection and no idea what she would do with all of it if she moved. And the message didn't say. Anna Maria figured she'd put the art in storage and live in one room somewhere, although the somewhere she would live was not apparent to her. But, she was not worried. "I had had a good life, I had a chance to live my art before I died. It was OK. So I packed these boxes."

In the meditative quiet and routine of packing up her house, Anna Maria says she was able to listen to God talking to her. And it happened. "It really was so loud and clear. He said 'I have something else for you.'" As if divinely led, the woman with no job and no money took the next step of a person who has a plan. She made an appoint-ment with a real estate agent to look at houses in Los Feliz, a lovely, pricey section of Los Angeles.

The agent had a list of five houses to show but recommended against one of them because it had been on the market and vacant for two years. The owner was said to be peculiar and stubborn about the asking price, which was more than Anna Maria would have wanted to pay if she did have a job, she said. They went to look at four of the properties but, unimpressed, Anna Maria asked to see the fifth – the problem house.

"We went into the neighborhood, where I'd never been before," she recalled. "It was like living in a park. It was so beautiful, full of trees. It was a block away from the city but you wouldn't know it. The weirdest feeling came over me. It was so strange." She didn't remember climbing the forty-three steps to the front door. But she remembered when the door was opened, "The stench coming out was so bad." And the house needed a lot of repair. Anna Maria walked around and saw the trees and was overcome. She immediately entered a very prayerful state, she said. When she emerged she told the agent that she wanted it.

The agent insisted that the owner's asking price was firm. Still, Anna Maria offered a bid that was $50,000 less. "I didn't have any money anyhow," she rationalized. "The house that I was in would have to sell for $300,000 less than what I paid for it. I wouldn't get a dime in a sale." So she just said "Fine, why not?"

Within days, the real estate agent called with the "good news" that the owner had accepted Anna Maria's offer. They set a date for closing. "So now I'm really a fraud," she said laughing at her audacity. "I still was not working and I couldn't tell anybody because nobody believed how bad I was doing." To get through those dark times, Anna Maria read inspirational books, particularly the writings of T.D. Jakes.

She continued to seek work, but gave her talent agent instructions that she would not go to any more auditions. "I couldn't take another audition and rejection," she said. "I told him if I ever worked in this industry again, God is going to have to bring me a job to my house cause I'm not going out. I'm not driving no where to be rejected."

Recalling the scene, her bold stand and the dialogue with her agent, Anna Maria laughed. "Usually," the word 'God' is not mentioned when you talk to agents," she said.

Days after giving those instructions, her talent agent called her with the news she was offered a role on the upcoming *Wayans Broth-*

ers Show. She figured it was just a guest spot. But it wasn't. The offer was a five-year contract as a regular on the series. And there would be no audition. They wanted her. She was back in business. Work at last! And, it was her birthday. "I hung up the phone and said God you know you have a sense of humor."

Still, what Anna Maria would be paid on the show would not be enough in time to buy the house. Settlement was in two days and she still didn't have the money to close. Feeling guilty and cowardly Anna Maria began steeling herself to call the agent and confess everything about how she went prospecting for houses knowing she had no income, and how even now with a job waiting for her she didn't have the money to close the deal.

But wait. This is Hollywood and time for the reversal of misfortune part of the script. At that moment in Anna Maria's life the script could have been entitled "How I Bought a House with No Money." The phone rang. It was the real estate agent calling with the "bad" news that the settlement had to be postponed. It seems there was a title irregularity on the property that had to be taken care of first. The agent apologized profusely. Anna Maria cupped her hand over the mouthpiece of the telephone, turned her head away and roared.

A new closing date was set for six weeks later but even with more time she still would be short $23,000. What happened next sealed Anna Maria's faith in a higher power, in God. Her accountant called serendipitously, just to let her know that if she ever had a need for any money she could borrow it from her pension fund. She hadn't known about that. She asked how much. He said he would check. A few minutes later he called back to tell her she could borrow up to the amazing amount of $23,000!

"Needless to say," Anna Maria noted, "I closed the deal and I told God 'I'll never doubt you again.' In all that I went through the only thing that lasted in my head was faith," Anna Maria said.

"Every time I get to the front door I think it was at my lowest point that I was able to buy a house. Each step I take up to the front door I have to step higher. Inside, there's another 25 steps to walk up. By the time I get in I have to pray because my heart is beating so fast. It is God who makes arrangements for me now."

"If you can raise a child alone
you can
run any corporation."

– Dianne Ziegler

two.
set your intentions

Dianne Ziegler wanted what a lot of people say they want: She wanted to be wealthy and she wasn't just saying it. She did not know how she was going to get there but she oozed determination and knew she had to change her life and change the way that mind behind those steady eyes worked.

Work as a real estate sales agent is a popular choice among many women seeking flexibility. It helps in life's juggling act to balance the job, the home and the active schedules of school-aged children. Now, sales does not typically provide the kind of big cash that made Donald Trump a billionaire but you can earn a living – if that's all you want. Dianne wanted more.

A single mom since her daughter, Margaret, was four years old, Dianne reasoned that if she was going to work for a living she should maximize the level of her return.

Slender and soft-spoken, the blonde with the studious eyes was born in Roanoke, VA. into a family of modest means and a strong work ethic. When her parents divorced, she was enrolled in a private Catholic school where the seeds of a desire for personal wealth were sown within her.

"I was the poorest one there," Dianne recalled. Her schoolmates owned their own horses and got private dance and piano lessons. Their mothers were homemakers and their fathers owned the major companies in town. By contrast, "My father worked for Norfolk Southern for forty years," she said. Rather than feel envious of her classmates' privileged situation "It created a dream for me," Dianne said. Ambitious and enterprising, she satisfied a desire to learn to play the piano by using her allowance to pay a friend to teach her.

Years later, when she entered the full-time workforce, Dianne turned her natural passion and empathy for people into a career in social work. It was a career that proved unfulfilling. "I was seeing so many people who didn't want to help themselves," she said.

She moved on. Her next job was with the Red Cross, overseeing blood procurement in the Roanoke area. She felt ineffective and continued thinking about how to create a more satisfying future. The idea came to her to buy a house for her and Margaret who by then was fifteen. "I felt I was wasting money paying rent." She did not qualify financially to buy in the neighborhood she liked. What's more, "the agent told me I never would." Angry and insulted, Dianne put her emotions to work for her.

Determined to get the house she wanted where she wanted it, Dianne scanned the real estate section of the newspaper and found one for sale by the owner in the neighborhood she liked. The two talked and the owner agreed to privately finance the mortgage, which allowed Dianne to afford the purchase. "I knew exactly what I wanted and I didn't want less."

That success started her thinking about a career change that would lead her to fulfill her childhood desire to be wealthy. She embarked on a personal course of study that included reading about Fortune 500 companies, noting how they operated and what made them and their investors succeed. This audacious spirit concluded that if she were going to meet her goal she would have to get into private industry; that's where the money was being made. As a way out of their jobs at the Red Cross and into something bigger, she and a co-worker took a real estate course. "I got out," Dianne said. Her co-worker stayed.

In 1985, at the age of 33, Dianne signed on with a real estate agency, deciding that if she was going to make money she would do it selling houses. "Selling real estate is much like being a boxer," says Dianne. "You are your own person. Your success or failure is a direct result of what you do or don't do," she says revealing her keen interest in the subject of success.

Dianne was committed to her goal of doing well and had both the courage and character to stay focused on the mission. She learned quickly that within the real estate industry, wealth was not in the retail sales she started out in, but in investment and development. She set herself on another long, self-directed course of study to understand that part of the industry. "I learned what it takes for a builder to build – location, price, etc. For the first couple of years I was just learning for free." But one lasting lesson came with a price tag that cost her $35,000.

In one of her duties as a sales agent, Dianne bought and sold lots for builders and received a commission on the sale. With each transaction she learned something new. In time, her hands-on experience provided her with invaluable step-by-step expertise about a process that builders profited from but did not know themselves. And like many women who are modest, even blind to their abilities, Dianne did not realize the value of her knowledge.

She went ahead and talked with a builder, offering to find property he could develop. In return she wanted a commission on the sale of the land and the houses she would sell that they would list with her. Dianne went forward and did due diligence over several months, studying the land, getting soil reports, checking local laws, titles and essentially getting the ground work covered. That done, she went back to the builder and asked to be part of the deal. On a verbal agreement she gave the builder all the information she had painstakingly learned. As the deal came together, she attended initial meetings but was gradually excluded and by the time the sale was completed she had been cut out altogether.

"I put in all that time and all that work studying the land and preparing it to sell to somebody when what I should have done was say no, I won't tell you where the land is unless the agreement is in writing. That's what I should have done but I went on blind faith that everybody was going to take care of everybody. I was thinking positive and believing that doing the work would do it for me."

Dianne could have put up a legal fight to force the builder to pay her. "I had a choice–I could have fought them in court for what was rightfully mine or I could have moved on." She chose to move on though not without resentment, she said. "It was a valuable lesson. Make sure you cover yourself so that you don't present a pie so someone can run off with it. Don't present the pie until they've paid for their portion. It was a very valuable lesson. Get your understandings written down."

The loss of the commission was a bitter pill to swallow. But something bigger and better was in store and fortunately Dianne made room for it by choosing not to spend time wallowing in the loss but focusing on her primary goal of building personal wealth. That was the same tactic that years earlier brought her the house in a neighborhood she was told she could never afford. Choosing to move on made room for the grandest of possibilities from the universal spiritual storehouse.

Dianne embarked on a new strategy. Now she was thinking like an entrepreneur. She decided she would become a real estate developer and builder herself. She identified successful people and studied them. One builder she watched was one of the largest in the world at the time. "I watched him and learned from him." She knew what she wanted to do. "I wanted to build houses."

Dianne was already prepared. She had sold subdivisions and learned how they worked. "You have to know what sells. You're using your own money and need financial skills and product knowledge. You need all your inner strengths. Selling is a job. Real wealth is in land. The question is 'Do you want to create a job or wealth?'"

Dianne had received enough career bruises and her vision for herself as a wealthy woman was so clear that taking these steps was a natural. She was not afraid to be aggressive, a characteristic generally discouraged in women but necessary in business if succeeding is part of the goal. Finally recognizing her own knowledge and experience as tremendous assets, Dianne got together with a trusted friend who was a lawyer with expertise in investment banking, and discussed pooling resources in a partnership. "I said why don't we build houses? I know where the lots are," she recalled. He agreed and the venture was on.

To pull together the cash to finance her end of the partnership Dianne turned her liabilities into assets and sold her house and her car. The car, an old Mercedes Benz, fetched $5,000 and the house she was told she could never buy brought her a $45,000 profit. "I thought I was rich." Dianne further reduced her expenses by leasing an apartment with a monthly payment lower than her mortgage had been and buying an inexpensive, low-maintenance car. She used the $50,000 profit as her share of the investment in the partnership.

"We pooled our resources, our gifts," she said. The first time out, the partners built two houses. The next year it was four. Now her company Parsell & Ziegler easily have thirty homes under construction at a time. They own an excavation company and build seventy-five residential homes a year, more than seven times the average number of houses constructed by the major builders in Roanoke who do ten a year.

Dianne works in a tough, competitive industry where a woman's natural instinct to help and do good might seem to be a liability. But it doesn't have to be if you operate with a basic principle "to do the right thing," she said. "You don't have to rip people off."

Dianne's story brings to mind the two popular schools of thought about how to acquire wealth: Be born into it or get lucky. Accomplishing the latter might mean marrying money, buying a winning lottery ticket or having a particularly spectacular night at Bingo. However, there is a far more deliberate way to acquire wealth and anything else we desire. "Set your intentions," Dianne says. "Have a goal. Have a desire," and whatever it is really work toward it, study it, learn about it inside and out and stay focused or as author Deepak Chopra advises, "Put your attention on your intention."

Dianne focused her mind and in a relatively short time succeeded, achieving wealth before she was forty. Her success was a result of ambition, hard work, maximum focus on goals and seeing an upside in an expensive lesson she never forgot.

To further illustrate her point of intention, Dianne recalled an incident in a house she'd just moved into. The washer and dryer were not working. She called a plumber who came over and after some time tinkering announced he could not fix the machines. She asked her partners, who were not experienced plumbers, to come take a look and in a few minutes they made the repair. When she asked how they were able to do what the plumber could not, their answer was one that resonated and she never forgot. They told her "We really wanted it done."

"When I work, I'm in rain, I'm in snow, I'm in mud—and I'm color coordinated."

— Alice E. Burley, construction site supervisor

three.
gumbo

If faith and dedication are the magic in accomplishing a seemingly impossible task, then we will soon see the return of the New Orleans of legend–especially if Amelia "Amy" LaFont and Lena Freeman have anything to do with it. I took a post Katrina visit to New Orleans. It unfortunately was my very first time in that storied city. Nothing really could have prepared me for what I saw. It was a mind numbing visual of blown away neighborhoods and a choking inventory of debris.

Amy LaFont served as my tour guide and host during my January 2005 visit. A drive through the devastated areas, particularly the lower Ninth Ward, was a painful vision of neighborhoods torn asunder, roofless houses, missing walls, bouquets of flowers in the rubble, a ghost town. Throughout the city, the façade of houses that appeared intact were marred with the shadows of water lines as high as 8 feet up from the foundation. Each was someone's home. And many of those who lived there were drawn back like migrating birds. But once you've returned where do you find the stomach to stay?

I met Lena Freeman and learned some of that answer. Mrs. Freeman told me that her first visit back to her house on Turo Street in the ninth ward came on October 27, 2005. Before the storm she evacuated with her son, daughter-in-law and grandchildren to Memphis. She thought she would be back quickly, three days at the most. But after a week or more passed depression set in. She was getting no information from the news on the condition of her neighborhood, her city. "Not knowing. Hearing only bits and pieces was hard," she recalled.

Mrs. Freeman, a round faced, friendly woman with brown skin and a look of satisfaction was sitting on her porch dressed in neat slacks and a crisp white blouse reading a newspaper when I noticed her. She said she has lived in New Orleans since 1979. She was a pantry worker who retired just a few years ago. After the storm hit, she said "I always knew I had to get back home."

Getting home was emotionally draining for her. She drove cautiously across the choppy road of the once active Claybourne Bridge passing through no longer recognizable neighborhoods to her own. She experienced a numbness from what she saw all around her. Finally at home, she stood in the doorway of her three bedroom house. The stench of rotting food in the refrigerator met her at the door. Furniture was water soaked. She cried. "Then, I looked over at the top of the dresser," she said. The small altar with a statue of the Blessed Mother and a crucifix that she kept there with family pictures was intact. "I found my strength. I knew the first thing I had to do was clean out all the mess."

A neighbor helped remove the freezer. Together with her husband and son they cleaned out the house then headed back to Tennessee to give the space time to air out.

The family returned in November to stay. For Mrs. Freeman, rebuilding her home was a critical first step in reconnecting to what is really important to her: a neighborhood of people who cared about each other. Our neighbors were always "checking up on each other," she said. "If someone is sick or we haven't seen someone for a while, we go by their house."

The houses are just a physical representation of what Lena Freeman and her neighbors throughout New Orleans ache to rebuild. The real rebuilding is of the invisible but palpable connection of the people one to another. In Lena's city, that is what rebuilding a neighborhood really is about.

And so it is for 32 year old Amy Lafont, a feisty young woman with high ideals who served as my host and guide for three days in her city. Restoring neighborhoods is what she has in mind for the devastated communities in her city. Her house is situated on high ground and escaped severe damage even as houses around her took on the impact of wind and water. "I prayed before the statue of Mary and thanked her for my life," said the mother of two boys, a cat and two dogs.

Amy describes her self as a "grounded idealist." It is an oxymoron that seems to work for her. She is fighting to assure schools are built. She sees them as a critical anchor for neighborhood restoration. In her job as construction manager for three charter schools, she is positioned to make it happen. Her mind's eye sees places abloom with colorful flowers and plants and children made happy and giddy from the beautiful sight.

Amy says she is of a family that counts ten generations of Cajun French on her mother's side who lived in New Orleans. Her grand-mom Erlene was a recognized genealogist who also did charts for other people. From a small child, people always told her she was going to do something special and whatever she wanted. Her something special may be bringing neighborhoods back from the dead. Amy says she wants to see through to completion the charter school building project. The plans call for creating a people's college that provides workshops on personal finance and on-demand learning. There's to be a school for kindergarten through eighth graders where children are the beneficiaries of "progressive excellence," critical thinking skills and social and emotional intelligence, she says.

"This is the work I was born to do," said the woman who laughingly describes herself as a secret agent for the forces of good. She certainly has made her intention clear. If the formula is true, Amy and Lena both will accomplish what they have set out to do in a city so devastated that recovery seems impossible.

"The beauty of a blessing is you never see it coming.
It always arrives on time and is exactly what you need
whether or not you knew you needed it."

four.
building a foundation

Peggy Logan is another of those urban pioneers who can see value where others see emptiness. Fortunately, her father handed her a hammer to hold during one of his many do-it-yourself projects. She was all of six-years-old. The power of what she could do with it stuck. Looking back, it was natural that the 54 year old real estate investor and renovator had become a first time homeowner when she was 22 and single. For Peggy, homeownership opened the door to a number of experiences she might never have had. She undertook all kinds of repairs from stripping paint to exposing original wood work to the total gut and renovation of houses.

But there came a point when a certain renovation was out of her control and she thought she was at the threshold of life's end. That was in 1999. Peggy discovered a lump in her breast. It was no big deal, she thought at first. She had cysts before. But after a medical examination she learned this one was different. It was cancerous and aggressive and needed treatment immediately. When she received the news "I nearly fell off the table," she told me.

The diagnosis could not have come at a more ironic time, in a way. Peggy was working out at the gym, kickboxing, exercising, eating well. She was in her third year as a single woman having divorced after 25 years of marriage. Life was good. And then, this. If the illness had come a year or so earlier, Peggy figures she might not have been able to handle it. But the marriage was over, she reasoned and she had moved on. And now, "I thought I was going to die but I was determined I wasn't going to go without a fight.

And she fought by applying useful distraction. During the period of treatment and convalescence, Peggy completed some seventeen do-it-yourself projects around her house. She redid furniture, set up furniture kits, and built a bar for the patio. "When I finished one project I went out and got another one."

Peggy also worked part time from home as a computer programmer. Some work days were seven hours long. "But in good conscience I only charged for four since it took me so long to do things." For nine months, she underwent an aggressive chemotherapy treatment that damages your joints.

"You do what you have to do to survive. I had property and had to keep it up. I had six at one time. It's a hassle but the only investment in which you can make $20,000 in four or five years," she noted. "Everybody has that will to live in them. We live in a society that celebrates life. Just laying down to die is not an option. It was about life. Even though I thought I was going to die I didn't worry about dying. I focused on living. Life becomes so precious when you are threatened with losing it. But the mind has got to want to do it and the body follows."

Peggy found therapeutic routine in the puppy she acquired the year before her diagnosis. "My day had to start at 6 am on a positive note walking the dog." She found the core of her strength in her belief in God. But she warns, that belief in God does not work as a sudden acquisition when you are ill. "You end up living on the systems you put in your life. It's what you practice on a daily basis in life that you live on when the chips are down. I knew how to pray so I got on my knees and I prayed. Meditation and prayer are a good body builder. You've got to have that relationship already. When things go horribly wrong that's the wrong time to be trying to find God. You have to build things in life. It is not all about money but build a foundation so you have something to draw on."

Peggy struck gold she did not know was there in her relationships with people. Cheryl Parker, her friend since 1st grade, cooked and helped her through the illness. "I was an independent person who didn't ask anyone for help. I had to learn to lean. I had to learn how to accept. You can't just make friends when you are sick. You've got to have that good relationship with you neighbor." When her car broke down, she waited at the bus stop to get to her radiation treatments for that day. Her neighbor saw her standing there and took her to that appointment and others. The woman from whom she bought artwork took her to the cancer support groups. The postman brought her mail to the door. She did all of her shopping through catalogs and 800 numbers which resulted in a friendship with the UPS driver on the route. He set up the tricycle she bought for her grandson. "How you treat people on a daily basis is what you are going to have to draw on in times of crisis," she said.

Peggy pays special notice to the irony that one of her biggest supporters during her treatment was her ex-husband who escorted her to all of her chemo appointments. "It reinforced in my mind that everyone comes into your life for a reason and you never know who God will send to help so you have to be mindful of how you treat everyone in your life."

five.
the gift of stress

When it comes to preventive maintenance, many of us attend to neither the house nor our self until there is stress. But used properly, stress can be a blessing if we look for the lessons. Cloaked behind the heavy fabric of disquiet, stress has a silk lining hard to discern at first. The trick is to create a preventive maintenance consciousness and summon the patience to ask the question "What is the lesson here?"

I began developing a preventive maintenance consciousness 'round the time I was doing the divorce thing. I came to realize that building this kind of consciousness can take a few years. It is built gradually by first stopping to examine how our reaction to stimulus contributes to the stressful outcomes in our life. It is an exercise in self-work necessary for strengthened emotional and physical health.

I found that a helpful way of looking at building that strength is to apply the analogy of the flight attendant's instructions. Hardly anyone who has flown more than twice pays attention to the preflight instructions about floating seat cushions and dangling oxygen masks. Those instructions are insightful applications not only for saving your life in the "unlikely event" of an aviation emergency but saving your life in general. The instruction says to secure the oxygen mask over your face first before attempting to assist anyone else, whether it is a loved one or a stranger sitting next to you. It is a powerful point to remember. You cannot help anyone else until you help yourself.

six.

pedestals and tiaras

There is something about the Victorian Age (1837-1901) that strikes a warm appeal for women–*which I think is ironic considering the 19th century was not the best of times for women if life as a first-class citizen was her idea of a good time.* Chastity belts with the steel girding and lace trim were a curious item of the time that seemed to hold a perverse appeal. Queen Victoria saw fit to promote the philosophy behind these instruments if not the instruments themselves as symbols of the virtue and essence of a woman. Velvet pedestals and lace motifs served as suitable accents and to this day remain of interest and desire for women.

But I wonder what was the real motivation behind Queen Victoria's thinking. *A tiara with too snug a fit? PMS? Menopause?* Whatever her reasons it had to be tough being Queen. *Who do you swap tales with about mood swings? The ladies-in-waiting?* Women who ache certainly want an antidote for the pain but first they need that emotional hug that says "I understand and you'll be fine." They want to, indeed, need to pamper away the bouts of 'unloved, unpretty, unworthy and misunderstood.'

Victoria created the pampered world that her wealth and influence could support and it is these same over-the-top fantasies about femininity that many women reach for when life has dealt a low blow. There is something viscerally appealing about the touch of delicate lace, the sight of billowing drapes, fine china, a tea service with special tongs for the sugar cubes, tiny teacakes, a special tray, dainty flatware, flowers, the flounce, the bounce, the pouf, the fringe, the bric-a-brac, perfumed air, ceremony and ritual. It makes one feel very special.

The therapy is in the frills and fussy detail. When life gets rocky you need to reach into your imagination and bring softness to the details. Retrieve the pedestal and sit upon it. Pull out the tiara and set it upon your head. *That steel girded chastity belt is starting to look pretty good right about then.* Your world is your castle. Everyone is your subject and all are posed in a deep, perpetual curtsy. You are Her Royal Highness. Love yourself that way. And for a little visual aid dress up a footstool or ottoman, grace a silver tray with a lace hanky, pearls, a tiara and a dainty tea cup and saucer. Keep them at the ready. When you are feeling low, pull them out, set them before you, relax and repeat "I am her royal highness. I am wonderful."

Here's to those pedestal and tiara moments!

acknowledgments:
thank you

Shelley
Betty Jean Murphy
Sonia Hobbs
Sarah Winchester
Yvonne Fisher
Alice Harrington
Dolores Ellis
Charleene Doverspike
Jocelyn Garlington
LaTanya Richardson
Dianna Brochendorff
Amelia LaFont
Lena Freeman
Anna Maria Horsford
Sarah Holley
Alice Burley
Dianne Ziegler
Alycia D. Taylor
Peggy Logan

for sharing your personal stories.

acknowledgments:
take them not for granted

The beauty of a gift is unawareness it is coming. I was hard at work at my computer one fine morning when the call came in from Shana Yarborough. She had a question. It was delivered so matter-of-fact it took me by surprise. "Are you interested in assigning publishing rights for two of your books?"

We had been introduced a few weeks earlier at a literary event. I learned Shana was a poet and the founder and CEO of a new publishing company called Writers Lair Books. I thought to myself then "Um, another indy pub company. Young people are so fearless, so naive."

I already had my experience running an independent book publishing company. It was daunting and I ran away. You can perform meticulous planning, but with any venture there are things you just don't know about until you are in it. A few years earlier, I had self-published the two titles Shana inquired about in that morning call. On April 1st, the week of the book promotion for one of them, I received notice that the distributor filed bankruptcy. I just knew it had to be a joke. But it wasn't. The courts held my inventory of books captive along with hundreds of other titles the distributor housed in a warehouse in Tennessee somewhere. That summarily ended my affair with book publishing and to this young woman I could only think: "Good luck kid."

Still, that morning on the phone, this young publishing entrepreneur piqued my interest. Assigning publishing rights for the books to her company meant my babies would get a second life in the marketplace.

I wouldn't have to do much more than freshen the content with new material, show up on the book tour *as the celebrated author*, read a few selections, sign a few copies and rake in the royalties. It was a no-brainer.

"Well, yeah, we can talk about it," I said answering her question. What she had to say over the next hour about her company, the marketplace, readers, her vision, the fit she saw for the book, and her plans for giving it reach were arresting. I said "yes," to her request.

I hung up and sat still to process what had happened the past sixty minutes or so. I had never spent that much time on the telephone on a business call, any call for that matter. The young woman with the calm, light, confident voice was a powerhouse of thought and delivery.

Shana Yarborough is one of the best examples of the bright lights within an emerging generation of young entrepreneurs who are continuing the age-old tradition of executing their dream with gusto. I guarantee you will be hearing much about this young woman and her publishing company.

And then there is Cassie Brand, Shana's "blessing" of an intern. In just a short time, this "mere intern" gained access to people who marketing pros take months to identify. The 18 year old freshman at Maryland's Goucher College is another great example of the focused, fearless minds I pray will dominate her generation of women. William Shakespeare might have said about this population: *The youths. Take them not for granted.*

about the author:
the renovating woman

A backed-up garbage disposal gave birth to *'Allegra Bennett the Renovating Woman™'*. Lively and humorously self-deprecating, Allegra describes herself as an avowed home repair ignoramus, until divorce and bad plumbing forced her to smarten up, demystify the workings of a house, and depend on herself to get the job done. She shared what she learned in broadcast commentaries, newspaper columns and three books. Hers is a seminal voice in the emerging trend of single female homeowners, who take on their own home re-pairs–*the Renovating Woman™ Movement*.

Allegra has been featured in newspaper and magazine articles and on home repair segments on local and national television shows. She makes appearances on *Home Made Easy*, a new show on the DIY Network, and on Baltimore station WBAL. Sought after for her expertise and authenticity, she became the spokesperson for the Baltimore Gas and Electric Consumer Energy Conservation Program in February of 2006.

In March 2005 Allegra launched *Renovating Woman Magazine*, a quarterly home improvement publication for women; and on April 1, 2006, she introduced the *Renovating Woman Do-it-HERself Workshops*.

Visit her web site at www.renovatingwoman.com